*no. 16 in a series of research reports sponsored by the NCTE Committee on Research

Children's *Poetry Preferences:

*A National Survey of Upper Elementary Grades

By Ann Terry
University of Nebraska

Reissuing this research monograph is made possible by a grant from the NCTE Research Foundation.

National Council of Teachers of English
1111 Kenyon Road, Urbana, Illinois 61801

CREDITS: Grateful acknowledgment is made to the following authors and publishers for permission to quote the poetry which appears in this monograph: For "Mummy Slept Late and Daddy Fixed Breakfast," from *You Read to Me, I'll Read to You* by John Ciardi. Copyright © 1962 by John Ciardi. Reprinted by permission of J. B. Lippincott Company / For "Lone Dog," from *Songs to Save a Soul* by Irene Rutherford McLeod. All rights reserved. Reprinted by permission of the author, The Viking Press, Inc., and Chatto & Windus, Ltd. / For "The Pickety Fence," from *Every Time I Climb a Tree*. Copyright 1925, 1929, 1949, 1952, © 1961, 1962, 1965, 1966, 1967 by David McCord. Reprinted by permission of Little, Brown and Co., and Curtis Brown, Ltd. / For "Poem to Mud," text copyright © 1969 by Zilpha Keatley Snyder from *Today Is Saturday*. Used by permission of Atheneum Publishers. / For "The Red Wheelbarrow," William Carlos Williams, *Collected Earlier Poems*. Copyright 1938 by New Directions Publishing Corporation. Reprinted by permission of New Directions Publishing Corporation / For "Shadows," copyright © 1968 by Patricia Hubbell from *Catch Me A Wind*. Used by permission of Atheneum Publishers / For "We Real Cool," from *The World of Gwendolyn Brooks* (1971). Copyright © 1959 by Gwendolyn Brooks Blakely. By permission of Harper & Row, Publishers, Inc. / For "Questions," by Marci Ridlon, from *That Was Summer*, published by Follett Publishing Co. Copyright 1969 by Marci Ridlon / For "Little Miss Muffet," by Paul Dehn, © *Punch*, London / For "December," by Sanderson Vanderbilt from the book *Creative Youth* by Hughes Mearns. Copyright 1925 by Doubleday & Company, Inc. Reprinted by permission of the copyright owner.

Library of Congress Catalog Card Number: 74-77997
ISBN: 0-8141-1535-2   NCTE Stock Number: 15352

National Council of Teachers of English

Research Report No. 16

The NCTE research monographs have made a distinct contribution to the field of English. Concerned with important issues, they have made significant findings available to the field. Most of the monographs have been marked by their attention to problems which researchers have long tried to answer.

Terry's study shows that children do demonstrate specific preferences in poetry, and that a judicious selection of particular poems by the teacher may enhance children's enjoyment of poetry. This study should increase teachers' awareness that children have strong likes and dislikes for poetry and that these likes and dislikes extend from form to content. Since the prime reason for including poetry in the school curriculum is to give students a chance to develop interest in and enjoyment of poetry, Terry's findings form the basis for helpful guidance in ways of introducing poetry to children.

Doris V. Gunderson
For the Committee on Research

ACKNOWLEDGMENTS

The study reported herein could not have been conducted without the help and suggestions from many friends at The Ohio State University. The writer is deeply indebted to Professor Charlotte S. Huck for her constant support and encouragement. Her insightful comments and willingness to listen made a study that seemed impossible at times possible. Several persons made helpful recommendations concerning the planning and implementation of the research design. For their significant contributions, the author gratefully acknowledges Professors Martha L. King, Jane Stewart, and Robert Emans. Following the data collection, numerous consultations were held with Professor Jack Barnett regarding the statistical analysis. His suggestions proved invaluable. A special note of thanks is extended to fellow graduate students who frequently gave their time and advice.

The writer is especially grateful to Mrs. Barbara Fincher and Mrs. Janet Hickman. The study would not have been completed without their efforts.

Several persons devoted hours of their time suggesting poems for the survey. The author is most appreciative to the following individuals for their assistance: Dr. Patricia J. Cianciolo, Dr. Helen K. Mackintosh, Dr. Joan Glazer, Miss Barbara Friedberg, and Miss Allaire Stuart.

Finally, many expressed the concern that teachers would not volunteer for a study of this duration. Therefore, to the almost six hundred teachers who eliminated this concern, the author is appreciative. To the final selection of teachers in Texas, Ohio, Florida, and Pennsylvania who conducted the study in their classrooms, the writer wishes to say thank you once again for the outstanding response and cooperation.

Lincoln, Nebraska   A.T.
February 1974

TABLE OF CONTENTS

LIST OF TABLES

INTRODUCTION

Glancing at a recent paperback book club catalog one becomes aware of the abundance of poetry books and records for children. Never before in the history of literature have such a quantity and variety of poems been published especially for children's enjoyment. The range of their content runs the gamut of human experience. Teachers and students can choose the funny, the nonsensical, the serious or the cynical. The realism that has become controversial in children's fiction has also entered poetry for children. Many modern poets are commenting on the social and environmental ills of our world. Pollution, street gangs, drugs, parental neglect, coping with loneliness are all themes that find their way into contemporary poetry for children.

Despite this new realism appearing in recent poetry, teachers continue to read to their classes the traditional poetry that they heard in their childhood. In a study of what teachers read to their children in the middle grades, Chow Loy Tom found the poem "Paul Revere's Ride" (1861) was shared more frequently than any other poem.[1] The survey also showed all but four of the forty-one poems most frequently read by teachers were written prior to 1928. Obviously teachers are ignoring the new poetry available to children today.

If teachers are concerned about developing children's continuing interest in poetry, the selection of poems becomes an important consideration. A modern children's poet, William Jay Smith comments: "How natural and harmonious it all is at the beginning; and yet what happens along the way later to make poetry to many children the dullest and least enjoyable of literary expressions? It is usually along about fifth grade in our schools that children decide poetry is not for them."[2] In the past, required memorization has stifled children's enthusiasm for poetry; however, an inappropriate or poor selection of poems may be just as deadly. Reading condescending or sentimental poems to students may completely turn them off. Choosing only the older, more traditional poems to read aloud may not inspire children's interest in poetry. And what about the "new"

---

1. Chow Loy Tom, "What Teachers Read to Pupils in the Middle Grades" (Unpublished doctoral dissertation, The Ohio State University, 1969).

2. Quoted in Virginia Haviland and William Jay Smith, *Children and Poetry* (Washington, D.C.: The Library of Congress, 1969), p. iv.

content? Do children enjoy the poems that reflect current societal problems? Huck and Kuhn suggest that poetry "should have relevance for today's child. 'The Village Blacksmith' was a favorite of our grandfathers, but it has little meaning for the child whose heroes work in space rather than under the spreading chestnut tree." Thus, they conclude that the poetry selected should be appropriate to the background of the child, the age level of the child and the age in which he lives.[3]

In thinking about the significance of selecting poems that interest students, the writer turned to studies that have considered elementary school children's poetry preferences. The search revealed the lack of a recent extensive survey that would help teachers when considering the new developments in poetry. In view of this apparent void, it seemed important and timely to assess children's response to all kinds of poetry. Therefore, cassette recordings were made of slightly over one hundred poems representing a variety of poetry available to today's children. The researcher sought to answer the question: *given the opportunity to hear both traditional and modern poems, various forms and content, and poems containing particular poetic characteristics, what would children prefer?*

Hence, the study reported herein surveyed fourth, fifth, and sixth grade students' poetry choices. Specifically, the research was conducted for the following purposes:

1. To determine what poems selected for the survey were most enjoyed by upper elementary students.
2. To analyze the most popular poems considering such characteristics as the (a) form, (b) content, (c) certain poetic elements, and (d) age of the poem.
3. To determine any relationships between children's choices and grade level, sex, and type of school setting (suburban, metropolitan, inner-city, and rural).

---

3. Charlotte S. Huck and Doris Young Kuhn, *Children's Literature in the Elementary School.* Holt, Rinehart, and Winston, Inc., 1968, p. 396.

CHAPTER 1

REVIEW OF THE LITERATURE

A plethora of reading interest studies were conducted during the 1920s and 1930s, including studies of children's interests in poetry. At one time, it appeared as though Teachers College at Columbia University produced a majority of the studies related to children's poetry choices. Reviewing these and other pioneer investigations from today's point of view, it seems that children were asked to respond to a variety of traditional or classic poems intended more for adults. The poems contained both language and content inappropriate for the elementary school age child. Recent studies have attempted to include poems that are more child-like in nature, and some researchers have made an effort to select modern poems along with traditional poems for children's reactions.

Richard Nelson, reporting the findings of his research (1966) comments: "Continuous study of children's poetry preferences is justified since, as long as poetry is being written, the last words have not been said."[1] However, if one considers a conclusion from the findings reported herein, much has already been said about children's interests. The results clearly indicate that students' poetry preferences have remained rather unchanged over the years. Thus, the following review of research findings, from the earliest studies to the present, tends to be of greater significance when we realize many of the investigators' statements apply to today's child and his poetry choices.

Children's Interest in Poetry

Early studies conducted by Wissler and Jordan indicated children had little interest in poetry.[2] Jordan, in analyzing the titles of 3,598 upper grade students' favorite books and magazines, reported both boys and girls showed little interest in books of poetry. However, both studies revealed children's interest in poetry increased with age, and girls indicated a greater rise in interest than boys.

---

1. Richard C. Nelson, "Children's Poetry Preferences," *Elementary English*, XLIII (March 1966), p. 251.

2. Clark Wissler, "The Interests of Children in the Reading Work of the Elementary School," *Pedagogical Seminary*, V (1897-1898), p. 532. Arthur M. Jordan, *Children's Interests in Reading*, Contributions to Education, No. 107 (New York: Teachers College, Columbia University, 1921), p. 89.

A pioneer investigation by Dunn questioned the large number of poetry selections included in the most commonly used reading series at the time (1921).[3] The contents of primers, first, second, and third grade readers were analyzed, and poetry was found to represent 51 percent of all the selections. Mother Goose rhymes, and poems by Christina Rossetti and Robert Louis Stevenson occurred frequently throughout all the series books examined. To determine children's interests in reading material, a panel of judges prepared a list of 31 sample poems and stories. These were then paired and voted upon by students in various geographical regions of the United States. The results revealed "the inferior position of the verse samples."[4] Dunn concluded this was a significant finding since poetry comprised a little over half of the selections in readers. Dunn also examined "poeticalness" and "verse form" to determine their relationship to children's choices. Finding their appeal almost negligible, she concluded they neither created nor hindered children's interest; therefore, other qualities must influence students' poetry choices.

A survey to discover what poems were enjoyed by children in the elementary grades was conducted by King in the early 1920s.[5] A total of 4,800 children in ten United States cities were involved in this study. Children listed two of their favorite poems and wrote reasons for selecting them as favorites. The five poems most preferred were (1) "The Children's Hour," (2) "The Village Blacksmith," (3) "Hiawatha," (4) "My Shadow," and (5) "Paul Revere's Ride." It is interesting to note that four out of the five favorite poems were written by Longfellow. The four most frequent reasons given by children for liking poems were (1) nature, (2) funny, (3) patriotism and loyalty, and (4) experience.

Grant and White, in their investigation of children's choices of reading material, refuted Dunn's conclusions concerning students' apathy toward poetry.[6] Information about children's preferences was obtained from public libraries in New York City and twenty classrooms located in various geographical regions of the United States. Discussing their findings, Grant and White indicate that children showed a substantial interest in poems when given a choice between prose and poetry. The two researchers also conducted interviews with children in the reading rooms of the libraries. When children were asked, "Do you like this book and why?" the

---

3. Fannie Wyche Dunn, *Interest Factors in Primary Reading Material*, Contributions to Education, No. 113 (New York: Teachers College, Columbia University, 1921), p. 69.

4. *Ibid.*, p. 39.

5. Cora King, "Favorite Poems for Children of Elementary School Age," *Teachers College Record*, XXXIII (May 1922), pp. 255-273.

6. Emma B. Grant and Margaret L. White, "A Study of Children's Choices of Reading Materials," *Teachers College Record*, XXVI (April 1925), pp. 671-678. Dunn, *Interest Factors in Primary Reading Material*.

most frequent response was "Because it is funny."

An extensive study of children's poetry preferences was conducted by Huber, Bruner, and Curry. A total of 50,000 children in grades 1-9 and 1,500 teachers participated in the two-year funded investigation.[7] To determine the poems considered appropriate for the various grade levels, the researchers asked for "opinions of expert teachers of poetry," and examined 900 courses of study along with the majority of the most commonly used textbooks. The poems occurring most frequently were included in the study. A record was kept to determine which poems the children in each participating classroom liked best or least. The final results of the study indicated that most poems were liked much better in certain grades than in others. Thus, the investigators suggested that proper grade placement was important when determining poetry selections for children. Other findings showed that in 1926, when the study was made, modern poems were not preferred over traditional poems, and "expert teachers of poetry" could not accurately judge the appropriate grade placement of poems. The four most universally liked poems were (1) "The Leak in the Dike," (2) "Little Orphant Annie," (3) "The Raggedy Man," and (4) "Somebody's Mother." A number of poems were disliked by children at all grade levels and Huber, Bruner, and Curry concluded the content of these poems was inappropriate for the elementary school age child.

Eckert investigated first, second, and third grade children's enjoyment of poems found in their school readers.[8] The study involved 200 students in the Pittsburgh Public Schools. Poetry selections for the research were obtained from both textbook and non-textbook sources. For each grade level, fifteen poems were put in groups of five and read to children. The pupils, in turn, told which of the five poems they liked best. Eckert's findings showed that in eight out of nine groups of poems, the poem taken from a non-textbook source had the greatest number of first choices. Other results indicated adults' choices of poems for children seldom coincide with children's choices.

Weekes' study was intended as a follow-up to the research conducted by Dunn.[9] Exploring the question, "What are the qualities that affect children's enjoyment of poetry?" her study attempted to determine (1) "the extent to which figurative language and involved sentence structure

7. Miriam B. Huber, Herbert B. Bruner, and Charles M. Curry, *Children's Interest in Poetry* (Chicago: Rand McNally and Company, 1927).

8. Mollie H. Eckert, "Children's Choices of Poems," *Elementary English Review*, V (June 1928), p. 182.

9. Blanche E. Weekes, *The Influence of Meaning on Children's Choices of Poetry*, Contributions to Education, No. 354 (New York: Teachers College, Columbia University, 1929). Dunn, *Interest Factors in Primary Reading Material*.

as factors of meaning affect children's choices of poetry; and (2) the extent to which actual experience as a factor of meaning affects children's choices of poetry." [10] A total of 412 sixth grade students from three large cities and six small communities were selected to participate in the study. Weekes randomly chose thirty-five courses of study from school systems for the purpose of determining poems for the investigation. After reviewing the courses of study, she concluded traditional poems appeared most frequently. The poems appearing second- and third-highest in frequency were "The Village Blacksmith" and "Daffodils," respectively. "Paul Revere's Ride" was observed in nineteen of the courses of study.

The final test material consisted of forty-one poems in original form, and simplified versions of seventeen poems adapted by the investigator. The purpose was to test the difference between comprehension of poems in the original form and comprehension of poems in the simplified form. The pupils also completed a questionnaire that was later used to determine the extent to which content within the children's range of experience affected their poetry choices. Weekes' findings suggest both figurative language and involved sentence structure make poems difficult for children to comprehend. She concluded both are factors affecting choice, since children appeared to choose those selections that were most readily understood. Experience, too, affected choice in Weekes' study. Children's preferences tended to reflect familiar or known experiences.

Helen K. Mackintosh conducted two related studies to determine children's interests in poetry. [11] Her enjoyment and concern for poetry stimulated a desire to learn more about children's preferences. The first study, reported in 1924, involved 68 fifth grade children in two cities in Iowa and Minnesota. The children heard one hundred selected poems, and ranked them on a five-point scale. The poems were read in groups of ten and arranged in order according to some general characteristic, such as ballad, narrative, etc. Certain qualities were distinguished and analyzed to determine their influence on children's choices: rhythm and rhyme, good story, excitement, adventure, dramatic interest, seriousness, humor, and dialect. The children were asked to help the teacher determine the best possible list of poems for fifth grade children. From the children's responses, a list of fifty poems was developed in order of popularity. Mackintosh concluded from the results that children's favorite poems are often not included in courses of study. She determined "the qualities previously neglected in choosing poetry for children are humor and dialect. A superior selection possesses not one but several characteristics

---

10. Weekes, *The Influence of Meaning on Children's Choices of Poetry*, p. 1.

11. Helen K. Mackintosh, "A Study of Children's Choices in Poetry," *The Elementary English Review*, 1 (May 1924).

that appeal to children, and probably contains an appeal to more than one grade level." [12]

The second study conducted by Mackintosh was more comprehensive than the first.[13] Children in grades 3 through 6 responded to four hundred poems selected on the basis of previous studies. Mackintosh employed an experimental procedure whereby several groups of children in grades 3 through 6 heard and responded to all of the poems over an eight-week period. A five-point scale was again used for recording children's preferences. The results of the study showed children chose poems that had the greatest number of interest qualities for them, such as child experience, dialect, humor, sadness, imagination, good story, and repetition. The findings indicated a variation from grade to grade in pupils' choices of poems; however, some poems were commonly liked by children at all four grade levels, and conversely, some were disliked at all grade levels. In comparing teacher-student poetry ratings, it was evident the two were not in agreement. Teachers tended to give higher ratings to the more traditional poems than their pupils. Teacher-student opinions coincided only when some modern poems were considered. Mackintosh discovered "literary merit was not necessarily an indication that a poem will be liked by children."[14] Children also showed little interest in the thoughtful, meditative type of poem.

First grade children's poetry choices were of interest to Bradshaw.[15] First graders in twenty-six Iowa and Illinois classrooms heard sixty poems selected from reading textbooks, previous research studies, and various courses of study. The poems were divided into six classes according to certain descriptors of content or style: (1) singing quality and rhythm, (2) about animals and nature, (3) about childhood activities and interests, (4) rhymes and jingles, old and new, (5) humorous poems, and (6) imaginative and fanciful. The children indicated a fondness for poetry. They enjoyed some old poems and some new poems, regardless of source, quality, and authorship. They liked funny poems, and poems that dealt with familiar experiences. Bradshaw noted that few courses of study included humorous poems. She also could find little agreement among authorities as to what poems should be introduced to first grade children.

Kangley conducted a study in 1937 for the purpose of determining the fundamental appeals in poetry that are operative with students at the

---

12. *Ibid.*, p. 89.

13. Helen K. Mackintosh, "A Critical Study of Children's Choices in Poetry," *The Elementary English Review*, I (May 1924), pp. 85-89.

14. *Ibid.*, p. 116.

15. Ruth E. Bradshaw, "Children's Choices in the First Grade," *Elementary English Review*, XIV (May 1937), pp. 168-176, 188.

junior high school level.[16] Approximately 328 eighth grade children participated in the study. Five judges and the investigator selected 120 poems which were grouped into categories corresponding to six appeals identified in poetry. Twelve poems were paired and read during each experimental period. Children were asked to name the best liked, next-best liked, least liked, and next-least liked poems. Kangley found obvious sound effect, commonplace subject matter, and obvious humor influenced children's choices. Straight didactic poems, poems with complex imagery, and nature poems received low ratings from students. Pupils completed an interest questionnaire, and the following reason was the most frequently given for liking a poem: "It was funny." The second most frequently stated reason was that the poem contained a rhythmic quality.[17]

Kyte, with the help of graduate students, undertook a study to determine the nature of elementary school children's reactions to poetry.[18] Published anthologies and elementary school reading texts were used to compile a list of poems. A panel composed of specialists in children's literature and elementary education selected 100 poems for evaluation using the criteria of literary merit and probable appeal to children. These were then classified by nature of subjects, mechanics of poetry, techniques of verse, pattern of the poem, kinds of poetry, and length of poem. Fifty poems were chosen from this classified list. The regular classroom teacher read the poems, and a total of 726 pupils, grades 3 to 8, rated the poems on a three-point scale and then wrote reasons for their evaluation. The findings from Kyte's study support previously mentioned conclusions determined by Huber, Bruner, and Curry, Eckert, Weekes, Mackintosh, and Kangley: Specialists in children's poetry cannot always determine the poems children will like; figurative language tends to make some poems difficult to understand, resulting in dislike for the poems; humor, dialect, repetition, rhythm, and familiar experiences are factors influencing children's preferences; some poems appeal to children at all grade levels and others do not.

The primary purpose of Avegno's investigation was to determine fourth, fifth, and sixth grade children's preferences for old and new poems.[19] Old poems were classified as poems published prior to 1900; new poems were defined as poems published since 1932. Poems were selected from

---

16. Lucy Kangley. *Poetry Preferences in the Junior High School.* Contributions to Education, No. 758 (New York: Teachers College, Columbia University, 1938).

17. *Ibid.,* pp. 138-141.

18. George C. Kyte, "Children's Reactions to Fifty Selected Poems," *Elementary School Journal,* XLVII (February 1947), pp. 331-339.

19. T. Sylvia Avegno, "Intermediate-Grade Choices of Poetry," *Elementary English,* XXXIII (November 1956), pp. 428-432.

anthologies, school readers, research studies, courses of study, and the investigator's knowledge of poetry. A final selection of 130 old poems and 120 new poems was determined. Fifty-five of the old poems were included in Mackintosh's *Critical Study of Children's Choices in Poetry* (1932). A total of 1,200 children in the New York City schools heard teachers read the 250 poems over a ten-week period. Students marked a five-point scale for each poem and gave reasons for their ratings. An analysis of the findings indicated that students preferred the new poems slightly more than the old poems. A comparison by Avegno of boys' and girls' poetry preferences showed the two differed only in degree. The students gave the following reasons for liking a poem: rhyme, musical tone, emotional tone, vocabulary, story, descriptions, religious aspect, moral value, everyday experiences, holidays, action, adventure, animals, nature, humor, imagination, difference, reality, and truthfulness. The most frequently stated reason for disliking a poem was failure to understand it.

Hofer conducted an experiment in her sixth grade classroom.[20] Opinion polls were taken after reading poems, some from the reading text and others selected by the investigator. Children were also invited to bring their favorite poems from home. Throughout the study, records were kept of children's reactions to poems. Students' responses indicated they enjoyed poems containing humor and a beat. The sixth graders enjoyed rhyming poems but showed little enthusiasm for poems containing repeated phrases. Limericks were well liked by all pupils, and verses about people received positive reactions.

One of the most extensive studies of children's reading preferences was conducted by Norvell and reported in 1958.[21] The investigation was in process for more than twenty-five years, and involved 24,000 children in schools throughout New York State. Pupils in grades 3 to 6 rated 1,576 prose and poetry selections by checking one of three statements: (1) very interesting, (2) fairly interesting, and (3) uninteresting.

The results of the study showed some poems were popular with both boys and girls; however, girls seemed to enjoy poetry more than boys. A comparison of their reactions to poetry in grades 3 to 12 showed that girls liked three times as many poems as boys. Norvell concluded, along with previously mentioned investigators, that experts on children's poetry (children's literature specialists, teachers, librarians, and anthologists) do not know children's likes and dislikes in poetry. Children ranked the following high in interest: poems of humor, animals, patriotism, Christmas, and Thanksgiving. Poems of nature, didacticism, fairies, and

---

20. Louise B. Hofer, "What Do Sixth Graders Really Like in Poetry?" *Elementary English,* XXXIII (November 1956), pp. 433-438.

21. George W. Norvell, *What Boys and Girls Like to Read* (New York: Silver Burdett Company, 1958).

high literary quality ranked low in interest. All of these, with the exception of literary quality, relate primarily to content. Findings suggested nonsense poems and limericks reached a high point of interest in grades 4 to 6. Norvell concluded,"nonsense makes its greatest appeal in the elementary grades."[22]

A study conducted by Nelson and reported in 1966 followed the methodology used by Eckert in 1927.[23] Forty poems for each participating grade level were selected from reading texts intended for the early grades. The investigator made a final selection of forty-five poems, fifteen at each grade level. Nine of these were included in Eckert's original study. A total of 385 first, second, and third grade children heard the poems over a three-day period. Thirty college students in a children's literature course were asked to select the poems they thought the children would enjoy most. The results of the Nelson study showed children liked poems containing action, near-nonsense humor, childhood experience, and a story line. The preservice college students demonstrated little success in predicting children's poetry choices. Nelson suggests, in view of this finding, "that children must be relied on themselves as the best judges of their preferences."[24] Eckert found the poems she selected were preferred over poems appearing in reading textbooks current in 1928. Nelson, in comparing his findings to Eckert's, concluded that reading texts current in 1966 included poems with greater appeal than texts published in 1928.[25] It is also significant to note that the poems taken from Eckert's study and included in Nelson's investigation were not particularly enjoyed by the children.

A number of conclusions may be drawn from this review of children's interest in poetry:

1.   Children are the best judges of their preferences.
2.   Reading texts and courses of study do not often include children's favorite poems.
3.   Students tend to prefer poems that contain humorous content; the nonsense of some limericks seems to be especially enjoyed.
4.   A poem enjoyed at one grade level may be enjoyed across several grade levels.
5.   Children do not enjoy poems they do not understand.
6.   Thoughtful, meditative poems are frequently disliked by children.

---

22. *Ibid.*, p. 65.

23. Richard C. Nelson, "Children's Poetry Preferences," pp. 247-251. Eckert, "Children's Choices of Poems."

24. Nelson, "Children's Poetry Preferences," p. 250.

25. Nelson, "Children's Poetry Preferences," p. 250. Mollie H. Eckert, "Children's Choices of Poems."

7. Some poems appeal to one sex more than another; girls tend to enjoy poetry more than boys.
8. New poems appear to be preferred over older, more traditional ones.
9. Literary merit is not necessarily an indication that children will like a poem.

Considering the above conclusions about children's preferences, it is evident the selection of poems can be critical in terms of children's enjoyment of poetry. The teacher is ultimately the one who screens the poetry selections and determines what poems children should hear. Therefore, the following section is devoted to studies concerned with the teacher's influence on children's interests in poetry.

The Teacher and Children's Interest in Poetry

Few interest studies have dealt extensively with the teacher's influence on children's choices, or with teachers' poetry selections. Mackintosh found that teacher and student poetry ratings were not in agreement.[26] Teachers gave higher ratings than students to traditional or classic poems. Norvell concluded teachers, librarians, children's literature specialists, and anthologists were unsuccessful at determining poems children enjoy.[27] The following two studies, however, suggest some conclusions about teachers' choices and their relationship to children's interests.

The purpose of Coast's study was to determine what poems most appeal to children and how teachers' choices influence children's taste in poetry. The investigation, conducted in 1920, involved children in grades 1 to 5 of the elementary school at the State University of Iowa. A week prior to the survey, teachers emphasized poetry in their classrooms, called attention to poetry books on shelves, and gave special demonstration lessons in poetry. Following this procedure, children were given a questionnaire regarding the preferred titles of poetry books and poems read at school or at home. Teachers also completed a questionnaire listing the ten poems they "most enjoyed teaching." The findings revealed an overlap between teachers' and children's choices, especially at grade one, and to a lesser degree in grades 3 through 5. "The poems upon which the teachers spent their energies and enthusiasm were in many cases the ones chosen by the children as their favorites," states Coast. Thus, she concludes: " . . . poems which teachers prefer are the ones most frequently chosen by children. This fact must surely strengthen the belief that the teacher's influence upon the literary tastes of her children is even more powerful than we realize."[28]

26. Mackintosh. *A Critical Study of Children's Choices in Poetry.*

27. Norvell. *What Boys and Girls Like to Read.*

28. Alice B. Coast. "Children's Choices in Poetry as Affected by Teachers' Choices." *Elementary English Review,* V (May 1928). p. 145.

Tom conducted a mail questionnaire survey to determine what teachers read to children in grades 4 through 6. The study was national in scope, including five randomly selected states from four geographical regions of the United States. A total of 582 questionnaires were returned out of the 1,020 mailed to elementary schools in Arizona, Delaware, Vermont, West Virginia, and Wisconsin. Findings showed one-half the poetry selections read by teachers in the middle grades were about nature (animals, birds, weather and the seasons) and people, places, and events (historical and patriotic). Less than 5 percent were fanciful poems. "The majority of the forty-one most popular poems were of the narrative form and all but four out of the forty-one were written before 1928." [29] Tom found the poem most often read in all three grades was Longfellow's "Paul Revere's Ride," a narrative poem published in 1861. Other frequently read poems were: "Stopping by Woods on a Snowy Evening" (Frost), "A Visit from St. Nicholas" (Moore), "Casey at the Bat" (Thayer), "Little Orphant Annie" (Riley), "Fog" (Sandburg), "The Village Blacksmith" (Longfellow), "My Shadow" (Stevenson), and "Hiawatha" (Longfellow). A poetry form, haiku, was also listed among the forty-one most frequently read poems. Other findings revealed one-third of the poetry read by teachers was taken directly from pupils' textbooks.

In summary, the following conclusions may be drawn from the findings of these two studies:

1. A teacher's enthusiasm and liking for a poem can influence children's choices.
2. Teachers tend to select the older, more traditional narrative poems to share with their children.

---

29. Chow Loy Tom, "What Teachers Read to Pupils in the Middle Grades" (Unpublished Ph.D. dissertation, The Ohio State University, 1969), p. 194.

CHAPTER 2

METHOD OF PROCEDURE

As previously mentioned, it seemed to the writer that an extensive study of children's poetry preferences was needed considering the new content of poems and the wide selection of poems written for today's young people. Therefore, the population of the survey presented here included fourth, fifth, and sixth grade public elementary school children from various parts of the United States. A multi-stage sampling plan was used to select a representative proportional sample by states, school systems, public elementary schools, and grade levels. Using the United States Armed Forces Institute's procedures for sampling, representative states were randomly chosen from four geographical regions of the country. A total of 1,000 letters requesting participants for the study were mailed to elementary school principals in the selected states of Pennsylvania, Florida, Texas, and Ohio. From an unexpected 598 positive returns, forty-five schools (fifteen in each of the four states) were randomly selected. This sample included fifteen classrooms at each of the three grade levels, a total of 1,276 children. To facilitate the analysis of data, a random sample of approximately ten children, five boys and five girls when possible, was drawn from each of the forty-two classrooms returning usable survey materials. The poetry choices of a total of 422 upper elementary age children were recorded and analyzed for the study.

Five consultants suggested poems for the survey: two professors of children's literature, two upper elementary grade teachers, and a pioneer investigator of children's poetry preferences, Helen K. Mackintosh. The consultants were asked to consider the form, content, poetic elements, and age of the poem when making their selections. A special form was developed by the investigator to help the consultants select representative poems for the study. After reviewing the poetry suggestions, the writer made a final choice of 113 poems. (See Appendixes A and B.)

The poems were recorded and duplicated on cassette tapes, making it possible for all 1,276 children to hear the poetry read by the same person. An announcer for a local radio station read and recorded the 113 poems. It seems significant to mention that this person was selected for the task because of his experience in reading poetry.

Two response instruments and the instructions for the study were field-tested with seventy-two children in grades 4, 5, and 6. While the two instruments correlated highly, one of them, illustrated with drawings of Charles Schulz's cartoon character Snoopy, elicited greater standard deviations per item. Therefore, an instrument based on a five-point scale ranking poems from "great" to "hated" was chosen for the survey. Accompanying illustrations showed Snoopy dancing for joy (for a reaction of "It's great!") looking pleased (for "I like it.") with ears at half mast (for "It's okay.") drooping (for "I don't like it.") and slumped in dejection (for "I hate it!"). See Appendix C for the text of the instrument.

Four questions appeared on the field-tested instrument; the following three proved the most discriminating and were used in the study: (1) How much do you like this poem? (2) Would you like to hear this poem again? (3) Could this be one of your favorite poems?

Children responded to each of the 113 poems over a period of ten days. They listened to ten to twelve poems per day, and no listening time was more than twenty minutes in length. Students heard each poem twice before making a judgment. Ten booklets containing the "Snoopy" instrument were provided for each child to mark his responses to the poems. The children wrote brief comments about the last poem heard each day, giving specific reasons for liking or disliking it. These comments were helpful in determining what poetic characteristics seemed to influence children's poetry choices.

Upon completion of the classroom survey, the teachers returned the children's response booklets along with a teacher questionnaire. The purpose of the questionnaire was to obtain information concerning the teachers' preference for poetry and their use of it in the classroom.

The analysis of data involved a review of the twenty-five most popular poems and the twenty-five most disliked poems among upper elementary age children, to determine the characteristics (type of poem, content, poetic elements, and age of the poem) that seemed to account for students' poetry preferences. The statistical measure chi-square was used to test the null hypotheses and the results from the following items on the teacher questionnaire were reported in frequency counts and percentage responses: (1) How often do you read poetry to your children? (2) Do children in your class write much poetry? (3) What is your main source for obtaining poems to use with your children?

CHAPTER 3

ANALYSIS OF CHILDREN'S POETRY PREFERENCES

A primary purpose of the survey was to determine what poems were most enjoyed by fourth, fifth, and sixth grade children. Table 1 lists, in order of frequency of "Great!" and "Liked" responses, the twenty-five most popular survey poems identified by the sample of 422 children.

Table 1

The Most Popular Poems

Title	Poet	f	%
Mummy Slept Late and Daddy Fixed Breakfast	John Ciardi	384	90.99
Fire! Fire!	Unknown	376	89.09
There was an old man of Blackheath	Unknown	372	88.15
Little Miss Muffet	Paul Dehn	368	87.20
There once was an old kangaroo	Edward S. Mullins	362	85.78
There was a young lady of Niger	Unknown	360	85.30
Hughbert and the Glue	Karla Kuskin	354	83.88
Betty Barter	Unknown	340	80.56
Lone Dog	Irene Rutherford McLeod	339	80.33
Eletelephony	Laura E. Richards	338	80.09
Questions	Marci Ridlon	337	79.85
Parking Lot	Marci Ridlon	332	78.67
The Ruckus	Dr. Seuss	332	78.67
The Pickety Fence	David McCord	320	75.82
We Real Cool	Gwendolyn Brooks	319	75.59
There was a young lady whose nose	Edward Lear	317	75.11
Adventures of Isabel	Ogden Nash	300	71.09
A Canner	Unknown	298	70.61
The Panther	Ogden Nash	298	70.61
Mean Song	Eve Merriam	294	69.66
Railroad Reverie	E. R. Young	285	67.53
Grizzly Bear	Mary Austin	281	66.58
Peter Piper	Unknown	280	66.35
I Wish That My Room Had a Floor	Gelett Burgess	274	64.92
Poem to Mud	Zilpha Keatley Snyder	273	64.69

Note: f = frequency, or number of students liking the poem; % = percentage of students liking the poem. To determine the number of students who reacted favorably to a poem, the categories "It's great!" and "I liked it" on the response scale were combined. See Appendix D for a list of poetry collections and anthologies containing the twenty-five most popular survey poems.

Another purpose of the survey was to analyze the most-preferred poems to determine what poetic characteristics seemed to account for their popularity. Four general characteristics or attributes were considered in this analysis: (1) form or type of poetry, (2) certain poetic elements, (3) content, and (4) age of the poem. Included under type of poem were narrative, lyric, verse, free verse, limerick, and haiku. Five poetic elements considered in the analysis were rhythm, rhyme, sound, imagery and figurative language. The content or subject matter of the poems included humor, familiar experience (everyday happenings), people, animals, nature, fantasy, historical events, adventure (action), and social commentary. Contemporary poems (those written recently, focusing on modern times) were distinguished from traditional poems (those considered children's classics, having stood the test of time).

Students' preferences for poems can readily be determined when one contrasts the most popular with the most-disliked poems. Table 2 lists the twenty-five poems identified as the most unpopular by the sample of 422

Table 2

The Most Unpopular Poems

		N = 422	
Title	Poet	f	%
The Red Wheelbarrow	William Carlos Williams	270	63.98
Haiku: "A bitter morning . . ."	J. W. Hackett	254	60.18
April Rain Song	Langston Hughes	250	59.24
The Forecast	Dan Jaffe	241	57.10
Dreams	Langston Hughes	231	54.73
Shadows	Patricia Hubbell	231	54.73
The Base Stealer	Robert Francis	219	51.89
Haiku: "A cooling breeze . . ."	Onitsura	219	51.89
Haiku: "What happiness . . ."	Buson	215	50.94
December	Sanderson Vanderbilt	213	50.47
Haiku: "How sadly the bird . . ."	Issa	212	50.23
A Song of Greatness	Chippewa Indian Song	210	49.76
Haiku: "Spring departing . . ."	Basho	207	49.05
Catalogue	Rosalie Moore	205	48.57
Fog	Carl Sandburg	202	47.86
Phizzog	Carl Sandburg	201	47.63
Silver	Walter de la Mare	199	47.15
This Is My Rock	David McCord	198	46.91
Haiku: "A cautious crow . . ."	Basho	194	45.97
The Pasture	Robert Frost	193	45.73
Who Has Seen the Wind?	Christina Rossetti	184	43.60
Rudolph Is Tired of the City	Gwendolyn Brooks	177	41.94
Street Window	Carl Sandburg	176	41.70
Haiku: "Little knowing . . ."	Issa	172	40.75
Buffalo Dusk	Carl Sandburg	170	40.28

Note: f = frequency, or number of students disliking the poem; % = percentage of students disliking the poem. The categories "I dislike it" and "I hate it!" are combined in this table. The haiku listed here are quoted in their entirety in Table 13.

intermediate grade children, who reacted with "I don't like it," or "I hate it" on the Snoopy instrument.

Type or Form of Poetry

An analysis of the twenty-five most popular poems shows the limerick to be one of the most-preferred types. Of the five limericks included in the survey, four are listed among the twenty-five best-liked poems. The form and humor seem to have built-in appeal for upper elementary children. "There was an old man of Blackheath" ranked third in popularity and is illustrative of the humor pupils found enjoyable.

> There was an old man of Blackheath,
> Who sat on his set of false teeth.
> Said he, with a start,
> "Oh, Lord, bless my heart!
> I've bitten myself underneath!"
> —Unknown

The students made written comments about why they liked or disliked the limerick: "There was a young lady of Niger/Who smiled as she rode on a tiger/They returned from the ride/With the lady inside/And the smile on the face of the tiger." The following comments taken from two children's response booklets illustrate why the limerick is special.

"I like it because I like limericks and it was funny." (boy, grade 4)

"I like the poem because it has so many rhyming words in it." (boy, grade 5)

Another popular form of poetry was the narrative. The poems ranking first and second among upper elementary children's preferences were written in narrative form: "Mummy Slept Late and Daddy Fixed Breakfast" and "Fire! Fire!" Other narrative poems mentioned among the twenty-five most popular poems were "Hughbert and the Glue," "Questions," "The Ruckus," and "Adventures of Isabel." The poem that tells a story seems to have a special appeal to children in grades 4, 5, and 6. Their favorite poem, "Mummy Slept Late and Daddy Fixed Breakfast" by John Ciardi, is an excellent example of a narrative poem written especially for children's enjoyment.

MUMMY SLEPT LATE AND DADDY FIXED BREAKFAST*

Daddy fixed breakfast.
He made us each a waffle.
It looked like gravel pudding.
It tasted something awful.

"Ha, ha," he said, "I'll try again.
This time I'll get it right."
But what I got was in between
Bituminous and anthracite.

"A little too well done? Oh well,
I'll have to start all over."
That time what landed on my plate
Looked like a manhole cover.

I tried to cut it with a fork:
The fork gave off a spark.
I tried a knife and twisted it
Into a question mark.

I tried it with a hack-saw.
I tried it with a torch.
It didn't even make a dent.
It didn't even scorch.

The next time Dad gets breakfast
When Mummy's sleeping late,
I think I'll skip the waffles.
I'd sooner eat the plate!
                              —John Ciardi

Among the twenty-five most unpopular poems shown in Table 2, the poetry form haiku appears seven times. A total of nine haiku were heard during the ten-day survey, beginning the second listening day and extending through the last. The investigator planned the nine-day sequence thinking exposure to a poetry form might influence children's choices. However, at the end of the classroom survey, it appeared most of the students held a consistent dislike for this form of poetry. Their written comments about the following haiku by Buson show their feelings about haiku in general.

---

*From *You Read to Me, I'll Read to You* by John Ciardi. Copyright © 1962 by John Ciardi. Reprinted by permission of J. B. Lippincott Company.

What happiness
Crossing this summer river,
Sandals in hand!
                    —Buson

"I hate it because its too short." (boy, grade 5)

"It was too short and I did not get nothing out of this poem."
(boy, grade 5)

"I know its suppose to be short but I don't like it because of that."
(girl, grade 6)

"It did not have any poem in it." (girl, grade 6)

"I like the words, but the way they sound is awful." (girl, grade 6)

"Because it gots no story behind it." (boy, grade 6)

"It doesn't make any sense at all." (boy, grade 6)

"It doesn't rhyme." (boy, grade 5)

"I don't like this poem because it is too short and I don't understand
it." (girl, grade 6)

This last haiku was intentionally chosen for children to write about, since it contains familiar content that might be particularly pleasing to students this age. Specifically, the investigator felt this would be a haiku children would enjoy if they enjoyed any at all. Many of the comments taken from the response booklets showed this to be true. However, the following statement by a sixth grade boy tends to summarize the feelings about haiku of the majority of children in the survey: "I liked this last one because it was about summer, but I still hate haiku."

Three qualities characteristic of the haiku can be identified from the children's comments as primarily contributing to their dislike for this form: (1) It is very brief. (2) It is sometimes difficult for children to understand. (3) It does not rhyme. Put these three qualities together and you have a form of poetry most children dislike.

Analysis of the most-disliked poems (Table 2) reveals another type of poetry upper elementary grade children appear to dislike. Free verse or poems containing no rhyme scheme appear throughout the disliked list; in fact, over half the poems contain no rhyming pattern, and many of these (with the exception of haiku), can be considered free verse. For example, "The Forecast," "Phizzog," "The Base Stealer," "A Song of Greatness," "Street Window," and "Buffalo Dusk" are all poems written in free verse.

Poetic Elements

An analysis of the most popular poems (Table 1) showed that three elements tended to influence children's choices: (1) rhyme, (2) rhythm, and (3) sound. As for the first element, rhyme, all twenty-five of the most-preferred poems among upper elementary students contain a rhyming pattern, and one poem, "Lone Dog," contains internal rhyme: "I'm a lean dog, a keen dog, a wild dog, and lone;/I'm a rough dog, a tough dog, hunting on my own." Rhyme seems to be a poetic element especially important to children. The results from the field study revealed that most of the fourth, fifth, and sixth grade students thought a poem was not a poem unless it rhymed. Written comments made by children participating in the national survey also illustrate a preference for poems containing rhyme.

> "I don't like it ("Mother to Son") because it doesn't rhyme." (girl, grade 4)

> "I like it ("We Real Cool") because it rhymes and it's real cool." (boy, grade 4)

> "I dislike this poem ("Foul Shot") because it doesn't rhyme." (boy, grade 4)

> "I like it ("Bam, Bam, Bam") because it rhymes and when it rhymes it sounds good." (girl, grade 6)

> "I like funny poems and ones that rhyme and I don't like this poem ("Stopping by Woods on a Snowy Evening") because it wasn't funny and it didn't rhyme." (boy, grade 6)

As mentioned earlier in the discussion about free verse, more than half the disliked poems (Table 2) contain no rhyming pattern; and analysis of reactions to haiku in the survey revealed that a primary reason for this dislike was absence of rhyme.

Another element influencing children's poetry choices is rhythm. The poem "The Pickety Fence" by David McCord is illustrative of the rhythmical quality children enjoy.

THE PICKETY FENCE

The pickety fence
The pickety fence
Give it a lick it's
The pickety fence

Give it a lick it's
A clickety fence
Give it a lick it's
A lickety fence
Give it a lick
Give it a lick
Give it a lick
With a rickety stick
Pickety
Pickety
Pickety
Pick
—David McCord

The poem "Railroad Reverie," another favorite among intermediate grade children, derives its appeal from the way rhythm is used to give the listener the feeling of the approaching train: "Far away, but growing nearer, growing nearer, growing nearer,/Coming closer, coming closer, coming closer all the while;/Rumble-rumble, rattle-rattle, clatter-clatter, clank-clank,/Chugger-chugger, chugger-chugger, and it reached the final mile." The poem contains the following refrain that appeared very popular with the students: "Catch-a-teacher, catch-a-teacher, patch-his-britches,/Patch-his-britches, catch-a-teacher, patch-his-britches,/Catch-a teacher—Woosh!" The comments that follow illustrate the children's enjoyment of the poem.

"I like this poem because I felt excited when I hear the train is coming and saying, "Here come the teacher!" (girl, grade 4)

"I like 'Railroad Reverie' because the way it is worded and rhythm and when you patch your teacher's pants." (boy, grade 5)

"I like the part where the train said patch your pants and catch your teacher." (girl, grade 6)

"I liked the words, the rhythm, and the excitement." (boy, grade 6)

The last most popular element for discussion is sound. A review of the twenty-five most preferred poems shows the following poems containing the quality of sound to be favorites: "Betty Barter," "Peter Piper," "A Canner," "Poem to Mud," "Mean Song," "The Pickety Fence," and "Railroad Reverie." Three of these poems are similar in nature, and some might refer to them as tongue-twisters. An example is this portion of "Betty Barter": "Betty Barter bought some butter./But she said, 'This butter's bitter!/If I put it in my batter,/It will make my batter bitter.'"

"Peter Piper" and "A Canner" are written in this same manner and depend on sound for their appeal. Another favorite, "Poem to Mud," also depends to a large extent upon sound quality for enjoyment.

POEM TO MUD

Poem to mud—
Poem to ooze—
Patted in pies, or coating your shoes.
Poem to slooze—
Poem to crud—
Fed by a leak, or spread by a flood.
Wherever, whenever, whyever it goes,
Stirred by your finger, or strained by your toes,
There's nothing sloppier, slipperier, floppier,
There's nothing slickier, stickier, thickier,
There's nothing quickier to make grown-ups sickier,
Trulier coolier,
Than wonderful mud.
                                        —Zilpha Keatley Snyder

An analysis of the twenty-five most-disliked poems revealed imagery was one of the least preferred elements. The most-disliked poem, "The Red Wheelbarrow" by William Carlos Williams exemplifies this statement.

THE RED WHEELBARROW

so much depends
upon

a red wheel
barrow

glazed with rain
water

beside the white
chickens
                                        —William Carlos Williams

Included in the "most-disliked" list were other poems relying primarily on the element of imagery: "Fog," "Shadows," "December," and several haiku. However, these poems also contain figurative language, and this element, too, appears to contribute to children's dislike of a poem. Many of the students indicated they disliked the following poem because they did not understand it or it did not make sense.

SHADOWS

Chunks of night
Melt
In the morning sun.
One lonely one
Grows legs
And follows me
To school.

—Patricia Hubbell

The results of a previous study conducted by Weekes indicated figurative language tended to obscure meaning, and thus contributed to children's dislike of certain poems.[1]

Content of Poems

A thread of humor seems to run through most of the preferred poems in differing degrees. Most of the poems shown in Table 1 contain obvious humor for both children and adults; however, few adults would consider the following poem, "We Real Cool," humorous, but many children did.

WE REAL COOL

The Pool Players
Seven at the Golden Shovel.

We real cool. We
Left school. We

Lurk late. We
Strike straight. We

Sing sin. We
Thin gin. We

Jazz June. We
Die Soon.

—Gwendolyn Brooks

1. Blanche E. Weekes, *The Influence of Meaning on Children's Choices of Poetry.* p. 40.

Other poems having particular appeal, such as certain limericks and "A Canner," "Peter Piper," and "Betty Barter," could be considered a form of nonsense: a type of humor that, according to Norvell, appeals to children in grades 4, 5, and 6.[2]

When children were asked to write why they liked certain poems, a frequent reply was, "It was funny." A similar finding was reported by Grant and White in 1925.[3]

Familiar experience also appears to be a determinant of children's poetry choices. Popular poems containing familiar content having possible appeal to a large number of children were "Mummy Slept Late and Daddy Fixed Breakfast," "Hughbert and the Glue," "The Pickety Fence," "Poem to Mud," and "Questions." The last poem, "Questions," seemed to be a favorite, probably because children could identify with the child in the poem.

QUESTIONS

What did you do?
Where did you go?
Why weren't you back
An *hour* ago?

How come your shirt's
Ripped on the sleeve?
Why are you wet?
When did you leave?

What scratched your face?
When did you eat?
Where are your socks?
Look at your feet!

How did you get
Paint in your hair?
Where have you been?
Don't kick the chair!

---

2. George W. Norvell, *What Boys and Girls Like to Read*, p. 65.

3. Emma B. Grant and Margaret L. White, "A Study of Children's Choices of Reading Materials," pp. 672-673.

> Say something now,
> I'll give you till ten.
> . . . .
> "See if I ever
> Come home again."
> —Marci Ridlon

The children's written comments about poems other than those appearing in Tables 1 and 2 indicate familiar experience influenced their preferences. For example, a sixth grade boy enjoyed the basketball poem "Foul Shot" because what happened to the player in the poem had also happened to him during a game. Another sixth grade boy liked the poem "Stopping by Woods on a Snowy Evening" because it reminded him of where he used to live in Michigan. Lastly, a fourth grade girl wrote this comment about why she enjoyed the poem "Daffodils": "I really dig flowers."

Familiar experience can work in an opposite way, too, causing children to dislike a poem because it reminds them of something unpleasant or tells about something they already dislike. The following examples illustrate this statement.

> "I don't like 'Foul Shot' because I can't make a basket when I play." (girl, grade 4)

> "I don't like the poem 'Daffodils' because I'm allergic to flowers." (boy, grade 4)

> "I don't like 'Stopping by Woods on a Snowy Evening' because I hate snow and I hate the woods because you might get poison ivy." (girl, grade 4)

Poems about animals appear throughout the list of twenty-five most popular poems: "There once was an old kangaroo," "Lone Dog," "Eletelephony," "The Ruckus," "Adventures of Isabel," "The Panther," and "Grizzly Bear." Thus, it seemed children favored content having to do with animals.

Age of the Poem

A review of the twenty-five most popular and the twenty-five most-disliked poems revealed the following information concerning children's feelings about contemporary versus traditional poetry.

Table 3

Comparison of Children's Preferences
for Contemporary and Traditional Poems

Popular Contemporary Poems		Popular Traditional Poems	
Little Miss Muffet	(1967)[a]	None	
Questions	(1969)		
Parking Lot	(1969)		
We Real Cool	(1959)		

Disliked Contemporary Poems		Disliked Traditional Poems	
Rudolph Is Tired			
of the City	(1956)	Fog	(1916)
December	(1925)[b]	Phizzog	(1930)
		Silver	(1920)
		Buffalo Dusk	(1930)
		The Pasture	(1936)
		April Rain Song	(1920)
		Who Has Seen	
		the Wind?	(1924)
		A Song of Greatness	
		(A Chippewa Indian Song)	

a. First publishing date.
b. The publishing date of this poem is not recent; however, the content is modern and the poem appears in several new anthologies.

   Three out of the four contemporary poems that were well liked by upper elementary children: "Little Miss Muffet," "Questions," and "Parking Lot," had been written within the past seven years, while "We Real Cool" is fifteen years old at this writing. No traditional poems were included in the children's list of twenty-five most popular poems. The following poem, "Little Miss Muffet," a parody, exemplifies a kind of contemporary content that appealed to students in all three grades, but especially in grade 6.

LITTLE MISS MUFFET

Little Miss Muffet
Crouched on a tuffet,
Collecting her shell shocked wits.
There dropped (from a glider)
An H-bomb beside her
Which frightened Miss Muffet to bits.
—Paul Dehn

   The children wrote about the poem "We Real Cool" by the Pulitzer-Prize-winning black poet Gwendolyn Brooks. This poem contains the current vernacular or slang popular among today's young people. Children's comments on this poem indicated their appreciation for the contemporary quality of the language.

"I liked it because it told about children today and what they do." (boy, grade 5)

"Because it sounds like something today instead of 20, 30, 40 years ago." (boy, grade 6)

"It uses neat words that kids like us use." (girl, grade 6)

"'We Real Cool' is a good poem because it is groovy, outasite." (boy, grade 6)

Table 3 shows that two contemporary poems were disliked: "Rudolph Is Tired of the City" and "December." Both poems discuss the social problems of city life and are presented from an adult's point of view. Another factor contributing to the dislike of the two poems may be some children's lack of urban experience. Rural and suburban children often are not well acquainted with city living, while children who have lived all their lives in the city may not identify with these particular experiences. "December" may have been disliked for still another reason. It is a very short poem containing no rhyme, and closely resembles the poetic form haiku.

DECEMBER

A little boy stood on the corner
And shoveled bits of dirty, soggy snow
Into the sewer—
With a piece of tin.

He was helping spring come.
—Sanderson Vanderbilt

The following eight traditional poems were unpopular among upper elementary grade children: "Fog," "Phizzog," "Silver," "Buffalo Dusk," "The Pasture," "April Rain Song," "Who Has Seen the Wind?" and "A Song of Greatness." After analyzing these poems, it seems a few broad generalizations can be made concerning why they were disliked: (1) The content was possibly not relevant for the age of the child or the age in which he lives. (2) The language may have been inappropriate for children in grades 4, 5, and 6. (3) Certain poetic elements such as figurative language and imagery or lack of rhyme may have contributed to children's distaste for these poems.

The students were asked to write comments about two traditional poems: "Stopping by Woods on a Snowy Evening" and "Daffodils." Children frequently said they disliked these poems because they did not make sense or they were too boring.

In conclusion, the majority of the written statements seem to indicate children in grades 4, 5, and 6 tend to prefer contemporary poems over traditional ones. Further evidence supporting this finding will be presented in the following chapter.

CHAPTER 4

FINDINGS

A number of hypotheses relating to children's poetry choices were tested using the statistical measure chi-square.* The following presents the results of analysis of the data.

Differences between Fourth, Fifth, and Sixth Grade Students' Poetry Preferences

The results of chi-square analysis of the twenty-five most popular poems suggest there is a relationship between degree of preference and grade level. Fourth, fifth, and sixth grade children seemed to prefer the same poems, but their preferences tended to differ in degree. Fourth graders showed higher observed frequencies for preferring certain survey poems than did children in grade 6. The only exception to this sequence is the poem "Little Miss Muffet" (see page 26). Sixth grade pupils indicated a greater preference for the poem than children in grades 4 and 5.

A similar analysis of fourth, fifth, and sixth grade students' responses to the twenty-five most disliked poems was conducted. The results indicated no significant differences in the amount of negative reaction among grade levels for twenty-two of the most disliked poems. Significant differences at the .05 level were shown for only three poems, "Fog," "Buffalo Dusk," and "Who Has Seen the Wind?"

Tables 4, 5, and 6 present the poems children in the three participating grades considered "Great!" The tables illustrate the overlap in preferences among grade levels.

In summary, it appears that fourth, fifth, and sixth grade children tended to agree in their liking or dislike for certain poems. There was, however, a descending degree of liking for poetry across the three grade levels, with fourth graders liking survey poems better than fifth graders; fifth graders, better than sixth.

---

*The formula used for the statistical measure chi-square is $\chi^2 = \sum\limits_{1}^{k} \frac{(o\text{-}e)^2}{e}$. Where χ^2 = chi-square, k = number of categories or groups, o = observed frequency in a category, and e = expected frequency within a category.

Table 4

Poems Considered "Great!" by Students in Grade 4

	No. of Students in Sample = 140	
Title	Frequency	Percent
Fire! Fire!	107	76.00
Mummy Slept Late and Daddy Fixed Breakfast	105	75.00
Hughbert and the Glue	97	69.28
There was an old man of Blackheath	91	65.00
Little Miss Muffet	89	63.57
Railroad Reverie	87	62.14
There once was an old kangaroo	87	62.14
Lone Dog	84	60.00
The Pickety Fence	83	59.28
The Ruckus	79	56.42
Betty Barter	79	56.42
There was a young lady of Niger	78	55.71
Mean Song	77	55.00
Eletelephony	76	54.28
Questions	75	53.57

Frequency = number of "Great!" responses
Percent = percentage of total sample

Table 5

Poems Considered "Great!" by Students in Grade 5

	No. of Students in Sample = 148	
Title	Frequency	Percent
Fire! Fire!	96	64.93
There was an old man of Blackheath	92	62.16
Mummy Slept Late and Daddy Fixed Breakfast	89	60.13
There once was an old kangaroo	82	55.40
Little Miss Muffet	75	50.67
Lone Dog	74	50.00
There was a young lady of Niger	73	49.32
Hughbert and the Glue	66	44.59
Questions	64	43.24
The Pickety Fence	63	42.56
We Real Cool	62	41.89
The Ruckus	61	41.21
Eletelephony	58	39.18
Parking Lot	58	39.18
Peter Piper	57	38.51

Frequency = number of "Great!" responses
Percent = percentage of total sample

Table 6

Poems Considered "Great!" by Students in Grade 6

Title	No. of Students in Sample = 134	
	Frequency	Percent
Mummy Slept Late and Daddy Fixed Breakfast	92	68.65
There was an old man of Blackheath	79	58.95
Little Miss Muffet	78	58.20
There once was an old kangaroo	71	52.98
Fire! Fire!	68	50.74
There was a young lady of Niger	64	47.76
We Real Cool	55	41.04
Lone Dog	53	39.55
Eletelephony	52	38.80
The Ruckus	52	38.80
Hughbert and the Glue	51	38.05
There was a young lady whose nose	47	35.07
Nancy Hanks	42	31.34
Adventures of Isabel	40	29.85
The Panther	39	29.10

Frequency = number of "Great!" responses
Percent = percentage of total sample

Differences between Boys' and Girls' Poetry Preferences

After tabulating "Great" and "Liked" responses, a chi-square analysis was conducted to determine whether there were any significant differences in boys' and girls' preferences for the twenty-five most popular poems. Table 7 presents the results and indicates there were no significant differences in preference for most poems.

The analysis of the data indicates significant differences at the .05 level in favor of girls' preferences for the following poems: "Hughbert and the Glue," "There once was an old kangaroo," "Betty Barter," "There was a young lady whose nose," and "Adventures of Isabel." Girls also showed a stronger preference for the poem "Nancy Hanks" than boys. There was a significant difference in favor of boys' preference for only one poem, "Lone Dog."

The writer noticed extreme differences in boys' and girls' reactions to the poems "The Swing," "Daffodils," and "Foul Shot." Therefore, a chi-square analysis was conducted for these three particular poems to determine the significance of the differences. The results indicated girls had a higher preference for "The Swing" and "Daffodils" ($p < 0.001$) while boys showed a stronger preference for the narrative poem about basketball, "Foul Shot" ($p < 0.001$).

Table 7

Boys' and Girls' Responses to Twenty-Five Favorite Poems

Title	χ^2 (degrees of freedom = 2)	Probability
Mummy Slept Late and Daddy Fixed Breakfast	5.28	N.S.
Fire! Fire!	1.40	N.S
There was an old man of Blackheath	.91	N.S.
Lone Dog	6.62	0.05 (B)
Little Miss Muffet	4.40	N.S.
Hughbert and the Glue	6.35	0.05 (G)
There was a young lady of Niger	1.21	N.S.
There once was an old kangaroo	8.62	0.05 (G)
Parking Lot	3.38	N.S.
The Ruckus	.17	N.S.
Betty Barter	6.52	0.05 (G)
Questions	1.59	N.S.
The Pickety Fence	.28	N.S.
We Real Cool	.39	N.S.
Mean Song	1.15	N.S.
There was a young lady whose nose	8.92	0.05 (G)
The Panther	5.66	N.S.
Grizzly Bear	2.21	N.S.
Adventures of Isabel	7.96	0.05 (G)
Railroad Reverie	.86	N.S.
Poem to Mud	1.04	N.S.
Peter Piper	2.26	N.S.
Nancy Hanks	11.02	0.01 (G)
I wish that my room had a floor	4.36	N.S.
A Canner	5.56	N.S.

Note: Probability: a statistical term referring to the proportion of times an event is expected to occur when considering all the pertinent and available data.
N.S. = not significant.   (B) = preferred by boys.   (G) = preferred by girls.

"Disliked" and "Hated" responses were tallied and a chi-square analysis was conducted to determine if there were any differences between boys' and girls' reactions to the most-disliked poems. As Table 8 indicates, significant differences between boys' and girls' responses were shown for seventeen of the twenty-five disliked poems. Boys indicated a stronger dislike than girls for sixteen of these poems. "Foul Shot" was the only poem receiving a more negative response from girls.

Eight disliked poems showing no significant differences between the two sexes were "The Red Wheelbarrow," "Shadows," "December," "Catalogue," "The Base Stealer," "A Song of Greatness," "Phizzog," and the haiku by Onitsura: "A cooling breeze and the whole sky is filled with pine-tree voices."

To summarize these findings, boys and girls demonstrated significant differences in preference for certain poems which differed in subject matter. Certain content, having more appeal to one sex than another, may

Table 8

Analysis of Boys' and Girls' Responses to Twenty-Five Disliked Poems

Title	χ^2	Probability
Haiku: "A bitter morning . . ."	15.85	0.001 (B)
April Rain Song	19.69	0.001 (B)
Red Wheelbarrow	4.43	N.S.
Haiku: "What happiness . . ."	16.08	0.001 (B)
Dreams	7.64	0.05 (B)
Shadows	3.76	N.S.
Haiku: "How sadly the bird . . ."	18.11	0.001 (B)
Fog	19.10	0.001 (B)
The Forecast	10.05	0.01 (B)
Haiku: "A cooling breeze . . ."	4.52	N.S.
December	5.96	N.S.
This Is My Rock	10.70	0.01 (B)
Haiku: "Spring departing . . ."	6.78	0.05 (B)
Haiku: "A cautious crow . . ."	12.22	0.01 (B)
The Pasture	9.88	0.01 (B)
Who Has Seen the Wind?	15.57	0.001 (B)
Silver	6.32	0.05 (B)
Catalogue	2.86	N.S.
The Base Stealer	.49	N.S.
A Song of Greatness	1.99	N.S.
Phizzog	.73	N.S.
Haiku: "Even as the snow fell . . ."	18.11	0.001 (B)
Daffodils	22.71	0.001 (B)
Foul Shot	23.88	0.001 (G)
December Leaves	13.02	0.01 (B)

Note: (B) = strongly disliked by boys.   (G) = strongly disliked by girls. See Table 13 for a complete list of haiku included in the survey.

influence preference. However, in most instances, boys' and girls' poetry choices were similar, and differed more in degree of liking than in the individual poems preferred. Relative to this, the findings suggest that girls tend to have a higher preference for poetry than boys.

Poetry Preference and Type of School Setting

Twenty-five popular poems among suburban, metropolitan, inner-city, and rural children were analyzed to determine any differences in preference. Table 9 shows the observed frequencies of suburban, metropolitan, inner-city, and rural children's favorable responses to the preferred poems, and also indicates the school setting where the highest preference for certain poems was expressed.

Chi-square analysis revealed significant differences in preference for nine of the poems: "Little Miss Muffet," "Questions," "Eletelephony," "Betty Barter," "Poem to Mud," "Lone Dog," "The Panther," "The Hairy Dog," and "Railroad Reverie." Suburban children indicated a

Table 9

Twenty-Five Poems Rated "Great" or "Liked"
by Children in Varied School Settings

Title	Number of Favorable Responses in Each School Setting			
	Suburban (N=142)	Metro-politan (N=124)	Inner-City (N=58)	Rural (N=98)
Little Miss Muffet	134*	107	38*	89
Mummy Slept Late and Daddy Fixed Breakfast	127	111	58	86
There was an old man of Blackheath	124	114	52	81
Fire! Fire!	123	116	52	83
There once was an old kangaroo	122	104	52	85
Hughbert and the Glue	120	101	47	86
Questions	120	94	56*	79
Eletelephony	118*	94	21	81*
Betty Barter	114	115*	47	73
The Ruckus	111	100	45	76
Poem to Mud	106*	74	27	66
Parking Lot	104	92	53	83
Lone Dog	103	106*	47	85*
We Real Cool	103	95	48	73
Adventures of Isabel	102	92	45	61
A Canner	101	82	44	69
Mean Song	100	77	41	76
The Pickety Fence	99	96	48	77
The Panther	99	99*	36	64
There was a young lady whose nose	98	88	55	76
The Hairy Dog	97*	72	33	70*
Rhyme of Rain	91	80	32	61
I wish that my room had a floor	88	84	43	61
Railroad Reverie	85	82	46*	72*
The Ceiling	83	75	34	59

Note: The asterisk indicates the poems that received a significantly higher number of "dis-liked" responses from children in a specific school setting.

stronger preference for "Little Miss Muffet," "Eletelephony," "Poem to Mud," and "The Hairy Dog"; and rural children's preferences tended to overlap those of suburban and inner-city children, showing higher observed frequencies of preference for the poems "Eletelephony," "Lone Dog," "The Hairy Dog," and "Railroad Reverie."

The twenty-five most-disliked poems were analyzed to determine any differences in negative reaction among children in the four types of school settings. Table 10 indicates the observed frequencies of suburban, metropolitan, inner-city, and rural children's negative responses to the disliked poems, and also indicates the school setting where the strongest dislike for a particular poem was expressed.

Table 10

Twenty-Five Poems "Disliked" or "Hated"
by Children in Varied School Settings

Title	Number of Negative Responses in Each School Setting			
	Suburban (N=142)	Metro-politan (N=124)	Inner-City (N=58)	Rural (N=98)
The Red Wheelbarrow	94	81	24	71*
April Rain Song	93	73	24	51
The Forecast	88	72	26	48
Haiku: "A bitter morning . . ."	80	77	24	73*
Dreams	85*	75*	24	47
Shadows	84	63	26	58
The Base Stealer	82*	64	26	47
Catalogue	79	57	20	49
This Is My Rock	76	58	18	46
A Song of Greatness	75	68	20	46
Rudolph Is Tired of the City	72*	52	16	37
December	71	69	21	52
Silver	71	59	23	41
Phizzog	70	69*	11	51
Haiku: "An old silent pond . . ."	69*	49	18	57*
The Pasture	69	61	19	41
Concrete Mixers	68*	40	12	35
Street Window	67	49	17	44
Who Has Seen the Wind?	65	58	16	45
Buffalo Dusk	65	49	16	41
Haiku: "A cooling breeze . . ."	63	75*	19	63*
Haiku: "Spring departing . . ."	63	63*	21	53*
Haiku: "A cautious crow . . ."	62	68*	14	42*
Haiku: "What happiness . . ."	62	71*	24	58*
Paul Revere's Ride	61*	37	25	23

Note: N = number of students. The asterisk* indicates the poems that received a significantly higher number of "disliked" responses from children in a specific school setting.

A review of the results presented in Table 10 indicates that metropolitan and rural children appear to have a strong dislike for haiku. Suburban children demonstrated an intense dislike for the poems "Dreams," "The Base Stealer," "Rudolph Is Tired of the City," "Concrete Mixers," and "Paul Revere's Ride."

Suburban, metropolitan, inner-city, and rural children's responses to the 113 survey poems were analyzed. The results revealed a significant relationship (p < 0.001) between degree of liking for the poems and the type of school setting. Inner-city children demonstrated the highest degree of favorable reaction to the poems. Children in rural and metropolitan school settings ranked second and third respectively in their liking for the poems. Among the four groups, suburban children liked the poetry least.

Table 11

Students' Responses to Contemporary Poems

Title	Frequency of Response (N = 422)		
	Great and Liked	Okay	Disliked and Hated
Little Miss Muffet	368	45	9
Questions	337	62	23
Parking Lot	332	61	29
We Real Cool	319	57	46
Emma's Store	231	118	73
For Blue	209	126	87
Bam, Bam, Bam	205	101	116
Southbound on the Freeway	186	116	120
Hydrants	168	118	136
Mother to Son	157	96	169
My Friend, Leona	156	149	117
A Different Way of Seeing	136	138	148
Concrete Mixers	111	150	161
December	93	116	213
Rudolph Is Tired of the City	89	156	177
The Forecast	60	121	241

N = number of students in sample

Table 12

Students' Responses to Traditional Poems

Title	Frequency of Response (N = 422)		
	Great and Liked	Okay	Disliked and Hated
Jonathan Bing	260	110	52
Nancy Hanks	250	106	66
My Shadow	223	125	74
Stopping by Woods	177	109	136
Daffodils	172	98	152
The Walrus and the Carpenter	162	151	109
The Swing	159	161	102
Paul Revere's Ride	156	120	146
The Village Blacksmith	148	145	129
Something Told the Wild Geese	122	138	162
Introduction to Songs of Innocence	111	142	169
Sea-Fever	109	160	153
Fog	98	122	202
Silver	97	126	199
The Pasture	91	138	193
Who Has Seen the Wind?	90	148	184

N = number of students in sample

A review of the findings reveals upper elementary children in the four types of school settings (suburban, rural, inner-city, and metropolitan) tended to differ in degree of preference. Inner-city children showed a higher rate of preference for the poems in the survey than metropolitan, rural, and suburban children; suburban children showed the fewest favorable reactions to the poetry when compared with the other three.

Preference for Contemporary versus Traditional Poems

Children's reactions to a total of sixteen contemporary and sixteen traditional poems from the survey list are presented in Tables 11 and 12. The frequency of the children's responses in the three categories (1) "Great!" and "Liked," (2) "Okay," and (3) "Disliked" and "Hated" is shown for each poem.

The results of chi-square analysis indicated a strong tendency among upper elementary grade students to prefer the more contemporary poetry included in the study. Students' written comments suggested that contemporary poems were more enjoyed because of their modern content and language.

Familiarity as a Factor in Students' Poetry Preferences

Participating teachers were asked to respond to the following item on the Teacher Questionnaire: "Were any of the survey poems already familiar to your children?" The following poems were mentioned most frequently by teachers: "Poor Old Lady Swallowed a Fly," "Eletelephony," "My Shadow," "Paul Revere's Ride," and "The Purple Cow." Using data related to students' reactions to poems that were already familiar, a one-sample chi-square was computed to determine if familiarity affected children's poetry choices. The results indicated students tended to prefer poems that were already familiar to them.

Relationship between Children's Home Settings and Regional Descriptions in Poems

Children's responses to three poems were analyzed: "Stopping by Woods on a Snowy Evening," "December Leaves," and "Sea-Fever." The setting described in each of the poems seemed characteristic of one or more of the regional settings represented by the four participating states—Texas, Florida, Pennsylvania, and Ohio. The results, however, showed no significant relationship between the regional flavor of the descriptions of nature in the poems and the children's preferences.

Table 13

Students' Responses to Nine Haiku

Haiku	Frequency and Percentage of Responses (N = 422)					
	Great and Liked		Okay		Disliked and Hated	
	f	%	f	%	f	%
(1) A bitter morning: sparrows sitting together without any necks. —J. W. Hackett	69	16.39	99	23.45	254	60.18
(2) How sadly the bird in his cage watches the butterflies. —Issa	107	23.35	103	24.40	212	50.23
(3) An old silent pond . . . A frog jumps into the pond, Splash! silence again. —Basho	146	34.59	113	26.77	163	38.62
(4) A cooling breeze— And the whole sky is filled with pine-tree voices. —Onitsura	107	25.35	96	22.74	219	51.89
(5) Spring departing Birds weeping, Tears in the eyes of the fish. —Basho	117	27.72	98	23.22	207	49.05

Table 13 (Cont'd.)

Haiku	Frequency and Percentage of Responses (N = 422)					
	Great and Liked		Okay		Disliked and Hated	
	f	%	f	%	f	%
(6) Little knowing The tree will soon be cut down. Birds are building their nests in it. —Issa	151	35.78	99	23.45	172	40.75
(7) A cautious crow clings to a bare bough, silently watching the sunset. —Basho	111	26.30	117	27.72	194	45.97
(8) Even as the snow fell Through it there came whispering A breath of spring! —Issa	156	36.96	100	23.69	166	39.33
(9) What happiness Crossing this summer river, Sandals in hand! —Buson	141	33.41	66	15.63	215	50.94

Children's Reactions to Haiku

Table 13 shows the frequency of various student responses to the nine haiku heard throughout the survey, as well as the percentage of responses in the "Liked," "Okay," and "Disliked" brackets. A one-sample chi-square revealed that a significant proportion of the students in all three grades disliked this form of poetry.

Relationship between Teachers' and Students' Favorite Poems

Teachers' preferences were also surveyed and compared with students' poetry choices. Data for this portion of the study were obtained from the teacher questionnaire. The teachers were asked to list the survey poems they found most enjoyable and wanted to remember for later use with children. Students' "Great" and "Liked" responses were compared to the teachers' favorite poems to determine if the choices were similar. The findings are presented in Table 14. A close look at this table shows that not all teachers identified students' favorite poems as ones they would like to share later. For example, one teacher wanted to remember the poem "This Is My Rock," yet this particular poem was liked by only 15.87 percent of the pupils. However, the majority of the teachers selected children's favorite poems. Supporting this statement, a chi-square analysis revealed that the poems chosen by teachers as favorites tended to also be popular with students. It is possible that some teachers were influenced by their children's enthusiasm for certain poems.

**Relationship between Poems Teachers Read
and Students' Favorite Poems**

Participating teachers were asked to identify their favorite poems to share with students. A number of poems mentioned by teachers were also included in the survey. Table 15 indicates children's reactions to these poems. According to the results, eight of the twenty poems appear unpopular with many students while two poems, "Lone Dog" and "Eletelephony," are among the most popular poems reported in the survey. Children's reactions to other poems appear very mixed. For some poems, such as "Paul Revere's Ride" and "The Village Blacksmith," the total number of students' responses is fairly evenly divided between the three categories: "Liked," "Okay," and "Disliked."

Other Data Obtained from the Teacher Questionnaire

The teachers responded to several items on the teacher questionnaire concerning the role or use of poetry in their classrooms. Table 16 shows the responses obtained from forty-two of the teachers to the following question: "How often do you read poetry to your children?" The results indicated one-half of the survey teachers read poetry occasionally to their children, and approximately another fourth (12 teachers) read poetry once a month. Considering that the school year extends over a nine-month period, this would suggest that 25 percent of the teachers read poetry to their children only nine times during the year, while 50 percent of the teachers read it even less!

A second item appearing on the questionnaire asked, "Do children in your class write much poetry?" Table 17 presents the teachers' responses to this question.

The majority of the forty-two teachers indicated their children wrote poetry occasionally or very seldom. One teacher made the comment, "We use it (poetry) more often for writing and art lessons."

A third item on the questionnaire asked the teachers, "What is your main source for obtaining poems to use with your children?" Table 18 presents the forty-two teachers' responses to this question.

The teachers' responses indicated 78.57 percent of them used poetry anthologies as a main source for obtaining poems, and less than half this number, 35.71 percent, mentioned basal readers. A personal poetry file was used almost as often as a reader with a total of 30.95 percent of the forty-two teachers indicating this as a source for children's poems.

In summary, it appears from teachers' responses that poetry is sadly neglected in upper elementary school classrooms. Students appear to have few opportunities to hear, read, or write poetry. Perhaps this finding partially explains why the results of this study are similar to those reported in many previous studies. If students throughout the years have had very little exposure to poetry, it seems only natural that their poetry choices would remain much the same. The comic is always enjoyable, but an appreciation for poems other than the humorous is developed through continuous experience with poetry.

Table 14

Students' Responses to the Teachers' Favorite Poems

Title	Frequency of Teachers' Responses (N=41)	Frequency and Percentage of Children's Responses (N = 422)					
		Liked		Okay		Disliked	
		f	%	f	%	f	%
Little Miss Muffet	8	368	87.20	45	10.66	9	2.14
Mummy Slept Late and Daddy Fixed Breakfast	8	384	90.99	24	5.69	14	3.32
Railroad Reverie	7	285	67.53	69	16.35	68	16.12
Southbound on the Freeway	7	186	44.07	116	27.49	120	28.44
Mother to Son	5	157	37.20	96	22.75	169	40.05
Nancy Hanks	5	250	59.24	106	25.12	66	15.64
The Ruckus	5	332	78.67	64	15.67	26	6.16
My Friend, Leona	4	156	36.97	149	35.31	117	27.72
Poor Old Lady Swallowed a Fly	4	256	60.66	137	32.47	29	6.87
Arithmetic	3	151	35.78	112	26.54	159	37.68
Bam, Bam, Bam	3	205	48.57	101	23.95	116	27.48
Eletelephony	3	338	80.09	72	17.06	12	2.85
Foul Shot	3	186	44.08	70	16.59	166	39.33
Lone Dog	3	339	80.33	56	13.27	27	6.39
Parking Lot	3	332	78.67	61	14.46	29	6.87
We Real Cool	3	319	75.59	57	13.51	46	10.90
Alligator on the Escalator	2	254	60.18	108	25.60	60	14.22
The Builders	2	208	49.29	132	31.28	82	19.43
Emma's Store	2	231	54.73	118	27.97	73	17.30
Every Time I Climb a Tree	2	242	57.34	105	24.88	75	17.78
Introduction to *Songs of Innocence*	2	111	26.30	142	33.65	169	40.05
The Panther	2	298	70.62	79	18.72	45	10.66
The Pickety Fence	2	320	75.83	70	16.59	32	7.58
Poem to Mud	2	273	64.69	93	22.04	56	13.27
Robert Who Is Often a Stranger to Himself	2	111	26.30	142	33.65	169	40.05
Sea-Fever	2	109	25.83	160	37.91	153	36.26

Table 14 (Cont'd.)

Title	Frequency of Teachers' Responses (N=41)	Frequency and Percentage of Children's Responses (N = 422)					
		Liked		Okay		Disliked	
		f	%	f	%	f	%
Stopping by Woods on a Snowy Evening	2	177	41.94	109	25.83	136	32.23
The Village Blacksmith	2	148	35.07	145	34.36	129	30.57
April Rain Song	1	78	18.48	94	22.28	250	59.24
Dreams	1	73	17.30	118	27.96	231	54.74
For a Dead Kitten	1	126	29.86	145	34.36	151	35.78
Fog	1	98	23.22	122	28.91	202	47.87
Four Little Foxes	1	134	31.75	158	37.44	130	30.81
The King's Breakfast	1	242	57.34	113	26.78	67	15.88
Loneliness	1	186	44.07	131	31.04	105	24.89
Mean Song	1	294	69.66	92	21.80	36	8.54
Modern Hiawatha	1	246	58.29	118	27.96	58	13.75
The Monkeys and the Crocodile	1	249	59.00	117	27.73	56	13.27
My Shadow	1	223	52.84	125	29.62	74	17.54
The Pasture	1	91	21.56	138	32.70	193	45.74
Pretty Boy Floyd	1	235	55.68	116	27.49	71	16.83
Silver	1	97	22.98	126	29.86	199	47.16
Something Told the Wild Geese	1	122	28.91	138	32.70	162	38.39
Swift Things Are Beautiful	1	143	33.89	154	36.49	125	29.62
The Swing	1	159	37.68	161	38.15	102	24.17
This Is My Rock	1	67	15.87	157	37.21	198	46.92
Vern	1	169	40.05	135	31.99	118	27.96
What Is Purple	1	204	48.32	122	28.91	96	22.75

Note: The categories "Great!" and "Liked" were combined to indicate the poems *liked* by the sample of 422 students. Similarly, the categories "Disliked" and "Hated" were combined to determine the *disliked* poems. f = number of student responses within a given category.

Table 15

Poems Teachers Indicated Were Favorites
to Share with Children

| | Frequency and Percentage of Children's Responses* (N = 422) | | | | | |
| | Liked | | Okay | | Disliked | |
Title	f	%	f	%	f	%
Lone Dog	339	80.33	56	13.27	27	6.40
Eletelephony	338	80.10	72	17.06	12	2.84
Poor Old Lady Swallowed a Fly	256	60.66	137	32.47	29	6.87
Nancy Hanks	250	59.24	106	25.12	66	15.64
The Monkeys and the Crocodile	249	59.00	117	27.73	56	13.27
Stopping by Woods on a Snowy Evening	177	41.94	109	25.83	136	32.23
Daffodils	172	40.76	94	22.27	156	36.97
My Shadow	223	52.84	125	29.62	74	17.54
The Swing	159	37.68	161	38.15	102	24.17
My Friend, Leona	156	36.96	149	35.31	117	27.73
Paul Revere's Ride	156	36.96	120	28.44	146	34.60
Arithmetic	151	35.78	112	26.54	159	37.68
The Village Blacksmith	148	35.07	145	34.36	129	30.57
Something Told the Wild Geese	122	28.91	138	32.70	162	38.39
The Toaster	118	27.96	145	34.36	159	37.68
Fog	98	23.22	122	28.91	202	47.87
Phizzog	95	22.51	126	29.86	201	47.63
The Pasture	91	21.56	138	32.70	193	45.74
Who Has Seen the Wind?	90	21.33	148	35.07	184	43.60
This Is My Rock	67	15.88	157	37.20	198	46.92

*The categories "Great" and "Liked" were combined to indicate the poems *liked* by upper elementary age children. Similarly, the categories "Disliked" and "Hated" were combined to determine the *disliked* poems. f = number of student responses within a given category.

Table 16

Frequency of Poetry Reading in Participating Classrooms

Frequency of Poetry Reading	Number of Teacher Responses
Every day	1
Once a week	7
Approximately once a month	12
Occasionally	21
Very seldom	1
Total Number of Teachers	42

Table 17

Frequency of Poetry Writing in Participating Classrooms

Frequency of Poetry Writing	Number of Teacher Responses
Often	3
Occasionally	26
Very seldom	13
Never	0
Total Number of Teachers	42

Table 18

Teachers' Stated Sources for Obtaining Poems for Classroom Use

Source	Number of Teacher Responses
Poetry anthologies	33
Basal readers	15
Personal poetry file	13
Periodicals	2
Library	1
Collections of children's poems	1
Language textbooks	2
New York Times articles	1

CHAPTER 5

CONCLUSIONS

Students in the upper elementary grades seem to have decided poetry preferences. The results of this study indicate that young people in grades 4, 5, and 6 choose particular forms of poetry as favorites, and their preferences tend to be influenced by certain poetic characteristics.

One of the most interesting findings of this research suggests that children's poetry choices have remained rather stable and consistent throughout the years. The results of this study are similar to those reported by poetry preference studies in the 1920s and 1930s. For example, humor, more frequently than any other poetic characteristic, seems to influence students' choices. If a poem is funny, children like it. Researchers King (1922), Grant and White (1925), Hofer (1956), and Norvell (1958), to name a few, came to this same conclusion.[1] Consistent with this finding, the limerick, a form in which humor predominates, seems to enjoy a lasting popularity with students. In contrast to their enthusiasm for humorous poetry, children show an intense dislike for sentimental or serious poems. Langston Hughes' poems "April Rain Song" and "Dreams" shared similar low rankings across all three grade levels. Adults may enjoy such poems, but upper elementary students appear turned off by them. Mackintosh's research (1932) supports this finding. The children in her study showed little interest in the thoughtful, meditative type of poem. Findings from other studies corroborate many of the findings of this study and show the stability of children's interests.

A closer look at the types of poetry students in the survey seemed to prefer reveals a strong liking for poems written in narrative form. The most popular poem in the survey was a humorous narrative by John Ciardi, "Mummy Slept Late and Daddy Fixed Breakfast." Karla Kuskin's "Hughbert and the Glue" was another favorite humorous narrative poem. Throughout the survey, as mentioned earlier, limericks consistently appealed to students. In writing about why they enjoyed the limerick

---

1. Cora King, "Favorite Poems for Children of Elementary School Age." Emma B. Grant and Margaret L. White, "A Study of Children's Choices of Reading Material." Louise B. Hofer, "What Do Sixth Graders Really Like in Poetry?" George W. Norvell, *What Boys and Girls Like to Read.*

"There was a young lady of Niger," they responded with "It was funny," and "It rhymed."

In contrast to the preferred poetry forms, others included in the survey enjoyed little popularity. The haiku in particular was strongly disliked by children in all three grades. To teachers who say their children write haiku and love it, this finding comes as a surprise. However, after hearing a series of haiku, the students in all three grades indicated a strong dislike for this form. Their comments suggest that they do not find listening to haiku enjoyable because the form is short, unrhymed, and sometimes too subtle for children to understand. One teacher responded on the teacher questionnaire, saying: "I was simply amazed! My children did not like the haiku. They didn't think they were poems."

Another form of poetry, free verse, was also unpopular with the students. It was consistently disliked, because children seem to want their poetry to rhyme. The most disliked poem, "The Red Wheelbarrow," is an example of free verse (see page 22).

Three poetic elements seem to be especially favored by students in grades 4, 5, and 6: (1) rhyme, (2) rhythm, and (3) sound. Poems containing one or all three elements seem particularly enjoyed. Kangley suggested from her findings in 1938 that obvious sound effects and rhythm influenced children's poetry choices.[2] Children in 1970 appeared to respond in the same way to these poetic elements.

Consistently throughout the survey, if poems were difficult to understand, they were disliked. William Carlos Williams used imagery in its purest form to create "The Red Wheelbarrow," the survey poem that children disliked most. Since "The Red Wheelbarrow" derives its greatest appeal from the mental image that is produced in the reader's or listener's mind, it may be that the elementary school age student has not acquired the kind of sophistication necessary for appreciating this type of poem. Poetry depending primarily on imagery for its appeal may interest only the older student or adult who has been exposed to a variety of poems and has come to appreciate subtler poetic devices.

The writer's analysis of survey poems, along with children's comments, led to the conclusion that figurative language tends to make some poems difficult for students to understand. Similar findings were reported by Weekes in 1929 and Kyte in 1947.[3]

There may be still another reason for students' responses to Williams'

---

2. Kangley, *Poetry Preferences in the Junior High School.*

3. Weekes, *The Influence of Meaning on Children's Choices of Poetry.* Kyte, "Children's Reactions to Fifty Selected Poems."

"The Red Wheelbarrow." Because the reader or listener must mentally complete this poem, it necessarily becomes a greater intellectual challenge. Many students in the survey sample may not have understood the meaning of the poem and consequently disliked it. It is possible that students who have not yet reached the level of formal operations in their intellectual development are not capable of doing the abstract thinking required to understand this poem.

Turning to the content that appeared most popular with pupils in grades 4, 5, and 6, the findings show that in addition to humor, familiar experience and animals were particularly enjoyable. As mentioned earlier, humor seems to be the favorite poetic characteristic among children. No matter how silly or ridiculous a poem may be, if it makes them laugh, they love it. Familiar experience, however, is not liked by all children all of the time. Individual students enjoy poems that talk about experiences they especially like. For example, if a child plays basketball and enjoys it as a sport, he likes the poem "Foul Shot." However, an unfavorable attitude toward the sport has just the opposite effect upon a student's response to the poem. If he does not play or like basketball, he tends to dislike the poem. Animals, the third-most-frequently-liked content, appear to have held special interest for children for a number of years. Norvell in 1958 reported that poems about animals ranked high in interest. [4]

The analysis of students' responses showed overwhelmingly that contemporary poems with modern content, in today's language, are preferred over traditional poems. The "old-favorites" referred to by Tom in her study, "What Teachers Read to Pupils in the Middle Grades," were not liked by students. Poems such as Frost's "Stopping by Woods on a Snowy Evening," Longfellow's "Paul Revere's Ride," Wordsworth's "Daffodils," and Sandburg's "Fog" received many unfavorable responses, making them among the least popular. The poems written in the current vernacular and containing up-to-date content appeared more relevant to this age group. In their written comments about one of their contemporary favorites, "We Real Cool," students remarked that the boys in the poem talked like they did.

After analyzing the most popular survey poems, it became evident to the writer that children's favorite poems usually contained more than one popular characteristic. For example the children enjoyed humorous narratives, limericks that rhymed, and the combination of rhythm and sound in poems. Mackintosh stated a similar conclusion in 1932 when she

---

4. Norvell, *What Boys and Girls Like to Read.*

suggested, "a superior selection possessed not one but several characteristics that appeal to children."[5]

The National Survey attempted to answer a number of specific questions about students' poetry preferences:

Do students in grades 4, 5, and 6 enjoy the same poems?

The responses indicated that students in all three grades tended to enjoy the same poems, but not to the same degree. As stated earlier, fourth graders showed higher observed frequencies for liking a poem than fifth graders; similarly, fifth graders indicated higher observed frequencies for enjoying a poem than sixth graders. The only exception to this was the parody on "Little Miss Muffet" (see page 26). Sixth graders showed a greater preference for this poem than pupils in grades 4 and 5.

This finding suggests to the writer that for children, poetry reaches its peak of interest at fourth grade and then begins to decline. Why does poetry become less appealing to students in grades 5 and 6? One could assume that as children approach the stage of formal operations in their thinking, their appreciation for poetry, with its potential for conveying subtleties of thought and feeling, might increase. Since a characteristic of poetry is that it can be read at several levels of complexity, there is no way of knowing whether the fourth graders were enjoying the literal level of a poem while the sixth graders may have been rejecting the figurative message. Still another assumption might be made. Older students may feel that poetry is childish and that consequently they have outgrown it. Teachers do not seem to help students raise their level of appreciation for poetry by consistently exposing them to this literary form. Therefore students tend to lose interest in poetry. They have never been given the opportunity to discover the qualities that make poetry interesting to persons no matter what their age.

Do boys and girls prefer the same poems?

The findings revealed significant differences in preference between boys and girls only for certain poems. Girls indicated a strong preference for "The Swing" and "Daffodils," whereas boys showed a high preference for a poem about basketball, "Foul Shot." Therefore, it appears that content with more appeal or meaning to one sex than the other may influence poetry choices. Boys' and girls' responses showed that the majority of their preferences were similar, differing more in degree than in kind. The findings indicated girls tended to have a higher preference for poetry than boys. It may be that girls turn more readily to books and poetry simply

---

5. Helen K. Mackintosh, "A Critical Study of Children's Choices in Poetry," p. 89.

because our society provides less for girls to do than for boys. Boys are part of Little League baseball teams and football teams; they attend sports events; even TV presents more programs that appeal to boys than to girls. Another reason for girls' liking poetry more than boys may be the feminine connotation that has been given this literary form in our culture. Poetry is for girls and not boys. It simply is not masculine for a boy to enjoy poetry.

Do children in different types of school settings prefer the same poems?

Analysis of the most-liked poems among inner-city, metropolitan, suburban, and rural students revealed the following results: (1) Inner-city children showed higher observed frequencies of preference than the writer expected for the poems "Little Miss Muffet," "Questions," "There was a young lady whose nose," and "Railroad Reverie." (2) Children in metropolitan areas showed a stronger preference for "Betty Barter," "Lone Dog," and "The Panther." (3) Suburban children indicated a stronger preference for "Little Miss Muffet," "Eletelephony," "Poem to Mud," and "The Hairy Dog." (4) Rural children's preferences tended to coincide with those of suburban and inner-city children, showing higher observed frequencies of preference for "Eletelephony," "Lone Dog," "The Hairy Dog," and "Railroad Reverie." Among the most unpopular poems, both metropolitan and rural children indicated a strong dislike for haiku; suburban students revealed a similar dislike for "Dreams," "The Base Stealer," "Rudolph Is Tired of the City," "Concrete Mixers," and "Paul Revere's Ride." It seems worth noting that two of the five poems most disliked by suburban children are about the city.

Children's responses to the most-liked and most-disliked poems revealed differences in degree of preference rather than in preference itself. Inner-city children showed the greatest enthusiasm for poetry, while rural and metropolitan-area children ranked second and third in number of favorable reactions to survey poems. Suburban students indicated the least liking for poems on the survey. The question becomes "Why do inner-city children enjoy poetry the most and suburban children the least?" Several inner-city students commented in their response booklets about how much they enjoyed hearing the poems. They indicated it was a break in the dull routine and something fun for a change. If one can conjecture from these comments, it may be that inner-city children have had less exposure to poetry than suburban children and therefore the opportunity to hear it became a unique and enjoyable experience to them.

Do students in the upper elementary grades prefer contemporary poems over traditional poems?

There was a strong tendency for students in grades 4, 5, and 6 to prefer contemporary poems over traditional poems. As mentioned earlier in this chapter, the language of contemporary poetry seemed to contribute to its appeal. Content of contemporary poems appeared relevant and meaningful, thus more enjoyable, to students in the survey, whereas many of the traditional poems had content totally divorced from their present-day experiences. In writing about "Stopping by Woods on a Snowy Evening," many students claimed they did not understand the poem. Content that had no meaning to these students probably contributed greatly to this reaction.

Does familiarity with a poem influence students' poetry choices?

The students tended to prefer poems that were already familiar to them. This finding certainly underscores the importance of teachers' reading poetry regularly to their children. Simply reading and sharing poems with students is the first step toward developing lasting interest in poetry.

Does familiarity with regional content in poems influence students' poetry preferences?

The writer thought that if children were familiar with the sort of natural setting described in a certain poem, they might enjoy the poem more. For example, the child who lives in a part of the country where it frequently snows might especially enjoy the poem "Stopping by Woods on a Snowy Evening." The research findings indicated this was not a valid assumption. Students living in Ohio and Pennsylvania seemed to dislike this poem just as much as those living in Texas and Florida.

Do students in the upper elementary grades enjoy the poetic form haiku?

A significant proportion of the students in grades 4, 5, and 6 indicated a strong dislike for this form. Teachers maintain that their children love haiku. When asked to elaborate about this, teachers reveal they are talking about students' *writing* haiku rather than hearing them read aloud. It may well be that children enjoy writing haiku but not listening to them. The haiku is probably more difficult for children to understand than any other form of poetry. When they write their own haiku the content is meaningful to them. However, when they hear haiku written by Japanese poets such as Basho and Issa, the form together with the content becomes a meaningless abstraction that they cannot relate to or understand.

Do teachers select children's favorite poems to remember and share later with other students?

The survey poems that teachers chose to remember for later use in their classrooms tended also to be children's favorites. It is quite possible that teachers' choices were influenced by students' enthusiasm for certain poems. However, the reason for this outcome does not seem as significant as the outcome itself. The very fact that teachers selected poems their students enjoyed and liked means next year's classes may have the opportunity to hear poetry that will interest them.

Do children tend to like the poems teachers read?

Twenty of the survey poems were among teachers' favorites to read to their classes. Eight, representing almost half of the selections, were disliked by a significant number of participating students. Two poems, "Lone Dog" and "Eletelephony," appeared among children's very favorite poems. These results seem to indicate that teachers in the upper elementary grades may need to seriously reconsider their poetry selections for classroom sharing.

How often are children in the upper elementary grades given the opportunity to hear or write poetry?

Approximately three-fourths of the teachers reported they read poetry to their children only occasionally or once a month. The writer considers this an appalling finding of the study, especially since all the evidence suggests that merely reading poetry aloud stimulates children's interest. A similar finding was revealed concerning the amount of time children spend writing poetry in the upper elementary grades. Thirty-nine of the forty-two participating teachers indicated their students wrote poetry occasionally or very seldom. One teacher said her students never wrote poetry. It is no wonder that children's poetry preferences have remained unchanged. Students have not been given the experiences with poetry that would raise their levels of appreciation and understanding of the various forms, content, and poetic elements.

Where do teachers obtain the poems that they read and share with their students?

More than three-fourths of the teachers said poetry anthologies were their main source for obtaining poems to share with students. Basal reading texts ranked second as a source, and a personal poetry file ranked third. Considering these results, it seems most important that college courses in children's literature provide undergraduate students with information about the wide variety of poetry anthologies available to teachers. Professors of children's literature should also help students establish criteria for selecting poems within these anthologies that will interest children.

The findings of this study of the information that has been obtained about children's preferences suggest that the teacher can be most influential in developing students' permanent interest in poetry. Therefore, the following chapter discusses in rather specific terms the implications of this study for the classroom teacher.

CHAPTER 6

IMPLICATIONS FOR TEACHING

It seems that sharing poetry with children during their elementary school years is an essential step toward developing permanent interest in this literary form of expression. This does not imply, however, that reading poems to students on a monthly basis will produce sustained enthusiasm for poetry. On the contrary, students need frequent exposure to poetry if they are to develop lasting enjoyment of its language and content. The results of this study indicate that after fourth grade, students' liking for poetry begins to decline. Therefore, the upper elementary grade teacher is confronted with a special challenge. To maintain and broaden children's interest, poetry should be shared in a variety of ways as a natural part of the on-going language arts program. The writer offers the following suggestions for making poetry an inherent part of the elementary classroom curriculum.

1. *Read and share poems with students throughout the academic year.* Choose a wide variety of poems. It is best if poetry reading occurs as a normal and expected part of the language arts program. A special day or time for poetry each week is not necessary. In fact, reading poetry every Friday afternoon, for example, may create an atmosphere of boredom rather than enjoyment. Care should be taken in selecting the poems to be read. A knowledge of students' interests and results of studies such as this one should benefit the teacher when choosing poems to share. (Later in this chapter, poetry selection will be discussed in greater detail.)

2. *Make books of poetry readily accessible to children.* Choose a wide variety of poetry books. A large number of poetry collections appear now in paperback and can be obtained rather inexpensively. Many of these have been compiled by persons who have studied children's interests and attempted to include poems students often enjoy. Studies show that students get enthusiastic about the books that teachers read aloud, and as a consequence, frequently choose to read them again. The same result can occur with poetry books. Make a point of choosing poems from the books available in the classroom, to read and share with students.

3. *Provide listening centers with cassette tapes and records.* A variety of cassette tapes and records of poems are available for children to enjoy. A listening center containing a choice of recorded poems with accompanying paperback books or filmstrips presents poetry to children in still another

enjoyable way. They can listen to their favorite poems over and over again if they wish. Students may want to record their own poetry selections and put them in the center. Adding sound effects to a poem such as "Poor Old Lady Swallowed a Fly" or recording a poem to music are activities that can get students interested in poetry.

4. *A rich poetry environment should stimulate some children's interest in writing their own poems.* Such writing should be encouraged by the teacher. Students may wish to share their poems. A class book of children's poems may be compiled and kept in the classroom library area. Some children may want to record their poems or set them to music for the listening center. Poems may be illustrated with photographs, slides, or pictures from magazines. An endless number of possibilities for sharing poetry are available to the creative, imaginative teacher.

To what extent are teachers already providing children with these kinds of experiences? According to the results of this study, teachers rarely read poetry to their students and seldom provide opportunities for them to write their own poems. It is no wonder then that students' poetry preferences have remained the same for a period of years. Children have not been given the opportunity to discover that poems other than the humorous or nonsensical can be enjoyable. If teachers provide experiences that get students actively involved in reading, sharing, discussing, and writing poetry, the level of their appreciation and response to poetry should be raised. Fourth and fifth grade students' preference for poetry might increase, rather than decline as this study has shown.

In planning experiences that get children actively involved in reading and hearing poetry, a teacher must carefully consider the selection of poems. If students have had little exposure to poetry, the wise teacher will begin with their expressed preferences. This study shows that students prefer to hear limericks, nonsense verse, and humorous narratives. Poems that rhyme and contain rhythm and patterns of sound are similarly popular. Children seem to enjoy the beat or rhythmic language of certain poems. "Railroad Reverie" and "The Pickety Fence" seem to be liked because they both contain this rhythmic quality.

Children frequently prefer poems about experiences that are familiar or enjoyable to them; however, *enjoyable* is the key word here. If the experience described in a poem is one that an individual student finds unpleasant or dislikes, the poem is consequently disliked for this reason alone. The differences shown in boys' and girls' preferences throughout the study are excellent illustrations of this finding. Boys tend to like basketball, and therefore liked "Foul Shot," a poem about basketball. Fewer girls tend to care for the sport, and consequently many disliked the poem. This finding seems to suggest that certain poems might be selected because they are especially appealing to one sex or the other. Since boys appear to lose enthusiasm for poetry as they get older, a selection of poems on subjects that will hold their interest seems quite important.

Should teachers select contemporary or traditional poems to read to students in the upper elementary grades? The findings of the survey indicate that students prefer contemporary poems to traditional ones. Students' survey responses indicated they enjoyed the language and content of the contemporary poems but frequently did not understand the language or content of some of the traditional poems. Tom (1969) found, however, that upper elementary grade teachers were primarily reading older poems such as "Paul Revere's Ride," "Daffodils," "Stopping by Woods on a Snowy Evening," "Fog," "Shadows," and "Who Has Seen the Wind?" [1]

It may be that teachers are sharing the poems they heard as children, thinking that today's children need to be exposed to these literary classics. However, students may never develop an appreciation for these poems if they encounter them before they have developed an enjoyment for poetry. First, students must like poetry; therefore, it seems important that teachers start with poems children want to hear. Contemporary poems containing relevant and meaningful content are more apt to interest elementary school students in poetry than the traditional poems currently being read. Teachers need to become better acquainted with poems that contain today's language and content. These should be included in the selection of poems that are read and shared with students throughout the school year.

The results of this study reveal that teachers' main source for obtaining poems to share with their students is the poetry anthology. Anthologies can be quick and easy reference tools; however, selection of poems is still a problem. Many poems found in anthologies are not the best to share when it comes to stimulating students' interest in poetry. A teacher must choose carefully the poems he feels his students will most likely enjoy. A particular anthology may also be kept too long as a resource. New editions and more current anthologies should be added regularly to a teacher's collection.

To this writer, one of the most interesting findings to come from the survey was upper elementary grade children's dislike for the haiku, not only because of its brevity and lack of rhyme, but also because they "don't understand it." As mentioned previously, teachers are amazed at this. They are presenting haiku in the upper elementary grades and asking children to write their own, although one wonders how many haiku teachers read to students before having them write one. This writer suspects more emphasis is placed on writing haiku than on reading them. It is quite possible that students enjoy writing their own poems but do not enjoy hearing Japanese haiku. The poems students write are meaningful to them

1. Chow Loy Tom, "What Teachers Read to Pupils in the Middle Grades."

because they are familiar with the content and language. But the implied emotion of haiku by Basho or Issa can be too subtle and complex for the upper elementary age child to understand. It would seem that Japanese haiku are not appropriate for the elementary school child. In agreement is James Moffett, who states: "Haiku have become so modish that they are now presented even to elementary school children. This is over-zealous teaching, I believe. The concreteness of the poems should not deceive us about their sophistication.2

Consistently throughout both the preliminary field study and the national survey, students indicated a strong preference for poetry that rhymed. While interviewing two participating teachers in the field study, the writer discovered that their pupils thought a poem could not possibly be a poem unless it rhymed. This finding raises interesting questions. Could it be that most elementary school age children are only exposed to rhyming poems? Or, in writing their own poetry, are they encouraged or required to make it rhyme, thus gaining the impression that all poetry should rhyme? A last possibility is that poetry is combined with the teaching of reading. It may well be that poems are used to teach children rhyming words or sounds as part of a phonics program.

Students frequently found poems containing the poetic elements of imagery and figurative language unenjoyable and sometimes difficult to understand. Because of the presence of these elements, the meaning of a poem becomes less obvious. It may be that the elementary school child who has not yet reached the stage of formal operations in his intellectual development is simply unable to comprehend the meaning of such poems. This suggests that teachers should consider the presence of these elements in the poetry they select to share with students. When imagery or figurative language are found throughout a poem, it may not be the best choice to read to elementary age students.

After considering all the findings of this study, one conclusion is paramount above all others. Poetry is a neglected literary form in most elementary school classrooms. The results reported herein indicate that teachers seldom read or share poetry with their students. When poems are presented, they are frequently inappropriate selections for stimulating lasting interest. Teachers' choices rarely reflect students' prior experience with poetry or their current level of enjoyment. Encouraging children to write their own poetry occurs as infrequently in the elementary school as reading poetry. It seems that if children are to enjoy and develop appreciation for poetry, it must first find its way into the classroom. Therefore, if the findings influence one teacher to do more with poetry than is presently being done, the unstated purpose of the survey will have been accomplished.

---

2. James Moffett, *A Student-Centered Language Arts Curriculum, Grades K-13: A Handbook for Teachers.* (Boston: Houghton Mifflin Co., 1973), p. 361.

APPENDIXES

APPENDIX A

FORM FOR POETRY CONSULTANTS

Note: Five consultants were asked to suggest poems for the study: two professors of children's literature, two upper elementary grade teachers, and a pioneer investigator of children's poetry preferences. Each consultant received a letter of explanation and the following form developed by the investigator. These were returned and used along with the writer's suggestions to determine the final selection of poems for study.

SUGGESTED POEMS FOR A NATIONAL SURVEY
OF CHILDREN'S POETRY PREFERENCES
IN THE 4TH, 5TH, & 6TH GRADES

I. *Types or Forms of Poems*
   A. *Verse* (merely a rhyme)
      Poem _____ Poet _____
   B. *Narrative* (a verse that relates a particular event or episode, or
                  tells a long tale)
      Poem _____ Poet _____
   C. *Lyric* (personal or descriptive poetry with no prescribed length
            or structure that possesses a singing quality)
      Poem _____ Poet _____
   D. *Limerick* (a nonsense form of verse)
      Poem _____ Poet _____
   E. *Haiku*
      Poem _____ Poet _____

II. *Poetic Elements*
   A. *Sound* - The alliteration or repetition of sounds in a poem, and
              onomatopoeia (the use of a word or words which
              imitate the sound they stand for).
      Poem _____ Poet _____
   B. *Imagery* - The representation in poetry of any sense experience,
               including images of sight, sound, touch, smell, and
               taste.
      Poem _____ Poet _____

C. *Figurative Language* - Refers to the use of metaphor (a figure of
speech in which one element substitutes
for another) and simile (a figure of
speech which makes a direct comparison
between two elements).
Poem _____ Poet _____

III. *Content of Poem*
A. *People*
Poem _____ Poet _____
B. *Animals*
Poem _____ Poet _____
C. *Humor*
Poem _____ Poet _____
D. *Everyday Happenings*
Poem _____ Poet _____
E. *Fantasy*
Poem _____ Poet _____
F. *Nature*
Poem _____ Poet _____
G. *Children's Experiences*
Poem _____ Poet _____
H. *Social Commentary and/or Commentary on Life*
Poem _____ Poet _____

IV. *Period*
A. *Traditional Poems* (poems considered as children's classics
having stood the test of time)
Poem _____ Poet _____
B. *Contemporary or Modern Poems* (poems written recently that
focus on modern or contem-
porary times)
Poem _____ Poet _____

APPENDIX B

POEMS SELECTED FOR THE SURVEY

Poems	Poets

First Day

Poor Old Lady Swallowed a Fly	Rose Bonne
The Toaster	William Jay Smith
Every Time I Climb a Tree	David McCord
April Rain Song	Langston Hughes
Lone Dog	Irene Rutherford McLeod
Dreams	Langston Hughes
Fog	Carl Sandburg
The Pickety Fence	David McCord
Eletelephony	Laura E. Richards
Bam, Bam, Bam	Eve Merriam

Second Day

Paul Revere's Ride	Henry Wadsworth Longfellow
Mean Song	Eve Merriam
Poem to Mud	Zilpha Keatley Snyder
Haiku: "A bitter morning . . ."	J. W. Hackett
The Base Stealer	Robert Francis
The Swing	Robert Louis Stevenson
The Goblin	Rose Fyleman
Little Miss Muffet	Paul Dehn
The Purple Cow	Gelett Burgess
We Real Cool	Gwendolyn Brooks

Third Day

This Is My Rock	David McCord
Betty Barter	Unknown
Arithmetic	Carl Sandburg
Galoshes	Rhoda W. Bacmeister
Who Has Seen the Wind?	Christina Rossetti
Haiku: "How sadly the bird . . ."	Issa
Mrs. Peck-Pigeon	Eleanor Farjeon
There was an old man of Blackheath	Unknown
Silver	Walter de la Mare
December	Sanderson Vanderbilt
Hughbert and the Glue	Karla Kuskin
Railroad Reverie	E. R. Young

Poems	Poets

Fourth Day

My Friend, Leona	Mary O'Neill
Jam	David McCord
Phizzog	Carl Sandburg
A Song of Greatness	A Chippewa Indian song transcribed by Mary Austin
Vern	Gwendolyn Brooks
Peter Piper	Unknown
Nancy Hanks	Rosemary and Stephen Vincent Benet
Haiku: "An old silent pond . . ."	Basho
People	Lois Lenski
There was a young lady of Niger	Unknown

Fifth Day

For a Dead Kitten	Sara Henderson Hay
Jonathan Bing	Beatrice Curtis Brown
Something Told the Wild Geese	Rachel Field
The Red Wheelbarrow	William Carlos Williams
Southbound on the Freeway	May Swenson
Rhyme of Rain	John Holmes
Haiku: "A cooling breeze . . ."	Onitsura
Fire! Fire!	Unknown
The Builders	Sara Henderson Hay
I Eat My Peas with Honey	Unknown
Too Blue	Langston Hughes
Foul Shot	Edwin A. Hoey

Sixth Day

I Woke Up This Morning	Karla Kuskin
Rudolph Is Tired of the City	Gwendolyn Brooks
What Is Purple	Mary O'Neill
Haiku: "Spring departing . . ."	Basho
The Hairy Dog	Herbert Asquith
The Ruckus	Dr. Seuss
Frog	Zilpha Keatley Snyder
The Panther	Ogden Nash
December Leaves	Kay Starbird
There was an old man with a beard	Edward Lear
Stopping by Woods on a Snowy Evening	Robert Frost

Seventh Day

Steam Shovel	Charles Malam
I wish that my room had a floor	Gelett Burgess
Loneliness	Janet Pomroy
Hydrants	Lee Bennett Hopkins
Bad Sir Brian Botany	A. A. Milne
The Forecast	Dan Jaffe

Poems	Poets
Haiku: "Little knowing . . ."	Issa
Swift Things Are Beautiful	Elizabeth Coatsworth
There once was an old kangaroo	Edward S. Mullins
Seal	William Jay Smith
Emma's Store	Dorothy Aldis
Daffodils	William Wordsworth

Eighth Day

Alligator on the Escalator	Eve Merriam
Catalogue	Rosalie Moore
Haiku: "A cautious crow . . ."	Basho
The Village Blacksmith	Henry Wadsworth Longfellow
Whispers	Myra Cohn Livingston
Buffalo Dusk	Carl Sandburg
Mummy Slept Late and Daddy Fixed Breakfast	John Ciardi
Otto	Gwendolyn Brooks
The Ceiling	Theodore Roethke
Some One	Walter de la Mare
Grizzly Bear	Mary Austin
Mother to Son	Langston Hughes

Ninth Day

Four Little Foxes	Lew Sarett
Pretty Boy Floyd	Woodie Guthrie
Parking Lot	Marci Ridlon
Adventures of Isabel	Ogden Nash
The Pasture	Robert Frost
Sea-Fever	John Masefield
A Different Way of Seeing	Marci Ridlon
A Canner	Unknown
Introduction to *Songs of Innocence*	William Blake
Haiku: "Even as the snow fell . . ."	Issa
The King's Breakfast	A. A. Milne
Shadows	Patricia Hubbell

Tenth Day

The Prayer of the Old Horse	Carmen Bernos de Gasztold
My Shadow	Robert Louis Stevenson
The Walrus and the Carpenter	Lewis Carroll
Questions	Marci Ridlon
Robert, Who Is Often a Stranger to Himself	Gwendolyn Brooks
Only My Opinion	Monica Shannon
The Modern Hiawatha	George A. Strong
The Monkeys and the Crocodile	Laura E. Richards
Street Window	Carl Sandburg
There was a young lady whose nose	Edward Lear
Concrete Mixers	Patricia Hubbell
Haiku: "What happiness . . ."	Buson

APPENDIX C

THE POETRY PREFERENCE INSTRUMENT

Note: Students participating in the study responded to the poetry selections by marking the following instrument. They were instructed to answer each question by circling the Snoopy cartoon that best illustrated their response to a poem. Students wrote comments about the last poem heard each day. They were asked to tell specifically why they liked or disliked the poem. The ten poems that children wrote about were selected because they were representative of certain forms, content, poetic elements, and eras.

POEM_____Railroad Reverie_____
  1. How much do you like this poem?
      It's great!   I like it.   It's okay.   I don't like it.   I hate it.
      (Accompanied by five cartoons of Snoopy in different moods)
  2. Would you like to hear this poem again?
      Oh, yes!   Yes.   I don't care.   No.   Oh, no!
      (Accompanied by the same five cartoons)
  3. Could this be one of your favorite poems?
      Oh, yes!   Yes.   I don't care.   No.   Oh, no!
      (Accompanied by the same five cartoons)

POEM_____Railroad Reverie_____

> Tell why you liked this poem.
> _____
> _____
> _____
> _____

> Tell why you disliked this poem.
> _____
> _____
> _____
> _____

APPENDIX D

POETRY COLLECTIONS AND ANTHOLOGIES CONTAINING THE MOST POPULAR POEMS

"Mummy Slept Late and Daddy Fixed Breakfast," John Ciardi

> Arbuthnot, May Hill, and Root, Shelton L., Jr., comps. *Time for Poetry*. Third general edition. Chicago: Scott, Foresman and Company, 1967.
> Ciardi, John. *You Read to Me, I'll Read to You*. Illustrated by Edward Gorey. Philadelphia: J. B. Lippincott Company, 1962.
> Larrick, Nancy, comp. *Piping Down the Valleys Wild*. Illustrated by Ellen Raskin. New York: Delacorte Press, 1968.

"Fire! Fire!" Poet Unknown

> Tashjian, Virginia A. *Juba This and Juba That*. Illustrated by Victoria De Larrea. Boston: Little, Brown and Company, 1969.

"There was an old man of Blackheath," Poet Unknown

> Brewton, Sara, and Brewton, John, comps. *Laughable Limericks*. Illustrated by Ingrid Fetz. New York: Thomas Y. Crowell Company, 1965.
> Larrick, Nancy, comp. *Piper, Pipe That Song Again*. Illustrated by Kelly Oechsli. New York: Random House, Inc., 1965.
> Larrick, Nancy, comp. *Piping Down the Valleys Wild*. Illustrated by Ellen Raskin. New York: Delacorte Press, 1968.

"Little Miss Muffet," Paul Dehn

> Dunning, Stephen, Lueders, Edward, and Smith, Hugh. *Reflections on a Gift of Watermelon Pickle . . .* New York: Lothrop, Lee & Shepard Company, 1967.

"There once was an old kangaroo," Edward S. Mullins

> Mullins, Edward S. *Animal Limericks*. Chicago: Follett Publishing Company, 1966.

"There was a young lady of Niger," Poet Unknown

> Brewton, Sara and Brewton, John E., comps. *Laughable Limericks*. Illustrated by Ingrid Fetz. New York: Thomas Y. Crowell Company, 1965.

Larrick, Nancy, comp. *Piping Down the Valleys Wild.* Illustrated by Ellen Raskin. New York: Delacorte Press, 1968.

"Hughbert and the Glue," Karla Kuskin

Kuskin, Karla. *The Rose on My Cake.* New York: Harper & Row, 1964.

"Betty Barter," Poet Unknown

Tashjian, Virginia A. *Juba This and Juba That.* Illustrated by Victoria De Larrea. Boston: Little, Brown and Company, 1969.

"Lone Dog," Irene Rutherford McLeod

Arbuthnot, May Hill, and Root, Shelton L., Jr., comps. *Time for Poetry.* Illustrated by Arthur Paul. Third general edition. Chicago: Scott, Foresman and Company, 1967.
Cole, William, comp. *The Birds and the Beasts Were There.* Illustrated by Helen Siegel. New York: World Publishing Company, 1963.
Larrick, Nancy, comp. *Piping Down the Valleys Wild.* Illustrated by Ellen Raskin. New York: Delacorte Press, 1968.

"Eletelephony," Laura E. Richards

Arbuthnot, May Hill, and Root, Shelton L., Jr., comps. *Time for Poetry.* Illustrated by Arthur Paul. Third general edition. Chicago: Scott, Foresman and Company, 1967.
Larrick, Nancy, comp. *Piping Down the Valleys Wild.* Illustrated by Ellen Raskin. New York: Delacorte Press, 1968.

"Questions," Marci Ridlon

Ridlon, Marci. *That Was Summer.* Illustrated by Mia Carpenter. Chicago: Follett Publishing Company, 1969.

"Parking Lot," Marci Ridlon

Ridlon, Marci. *That Was Summer.* Illustrated by Mia Carpenter. Chicago: Follett Publishing Company, 1969.

"The Ruckus," Dr. Seuss

Schiller, Andrew, et al. *Language and How to Use It*, Book Three. Glenview, Illinois: Scott, Foresman and Company, 1969.

"We Real Cool," Gwendolyn Brooks

Adoff, Arnold, comp. *I Am the Darker Brother.* Illustrated by Benny Andrews. New York: Macmillan Publishing Co., Inc., 1968.

Bontemps, Arna, comp. *Hold Fast to Dreams*. Chicago: Follett Publishing Company, 1969.

Larrick, Nancy, comp. *On City Streets*. Illustrated by David Sagarin. New York: M. Evans and Company, 1968.

"The Pickety Fence," David McCord

McCord, David. *Every Time I Climb a Tree*. Illustrated by Marc Simont. New York: Little, Brown and Company, 1967.

"There was a young lady whose nose," Edward Lear

Brewton, Sara, and Brewton, John E., comps. *Laughable Limericks*. Illustrated by Ingrid Fetz. New York: Thomas Y. Crowell Company, 1965.

"Adventures of Isabel," Ogden Nash

Larrick, Nancy, comp. *Piper, Pipe That Song Again*. Illustrated by Kelly Oechsli. New York: Random House, Inc., 1965.

Larrick, Nancy, comp. *Piping Down the Valleys Wild*. Illustrated by Ellen Raskin. New York: Delacorte Press, 1968.

"A Canner . . . ," Carolyn Wells

Brewton, Sara, and Brewton, John, comps. *Laughable Limericks*. Illustrated by Ingrid Fetz. New York: Thomas Y. Crowell Company, 1965.

"The Panther," Ogden Nash

Cole, William, comp. *The Birds and the Beasts Were There*. Illustrated by Helen Siegel. New York: World Publishing Company, 1963.

"Mean Song," Eve Merriam

Merriam, Eve. *There Is No Rhyme for Silver*. Illustrated by Joseph Schindelman. New York: Atheneum Publishers, 1967.

"Railroad Reverie," E. R. Young

McGovern, Ann, comp. *The Arrow Book of Poetry*. Illustrated by Grisha Dotzenko. New York: Scholastic Book Services, 1965.

"Grizzly Bear," Mary Austin

Arbuthnot, May Hill, and Root, Shelton L., Jr., comps. *Time for Poetry*. Illustrated by Arthur Paul. Third general edition. Chicago: Scott, Foresman and Company, 1967.

Larrick, Nancy, comp. *Piper, Pipe That Song Again*. Illustrated by Kelly Oechsli. New York: Random House, Inc., 1965.

Larrick, Nancy, comp. *Piping Down the Valleys Wild.* Illustrated by Ellen Raskin. New York: Delacorte Press, 1968.

"Peter Piper picked a peck of pickled peppers . . . ," Poet Unknown

Withers, Carl, comp. *A Rocket in My Pocket.* Illustrated by Susanne Suba. New York: Holt, Rinehart and Winston, 1948.

"I wish that my room had a floor" ("Relativity and Levitation"), Gelett Burgess

Brewton, Sara, and Brewton, John E., comps. *Laughable Limericks.* Illustrated by Ingrid Fetz. New York: Thomas Y. Crowell Company, 1965.

Larrick, Nancy, comp. *Piper, Pipe That Song Again.* Illustrated by Kelly Oechsli. New York: Random House, Inc., 1965.

"Poem to Mud," Zilpha Keatley Snyder

Snyder, Zilpha Keatley. *Today Is Saturday.* Illustrated by John Arms. New York: Atheneum Publishers, 1969.

SELECTED BIBLIOGRAPHY

Books

Dunn, Fannie Wyche. *Interest Factors in Primary Reading Material.* Contributions to Education, No. 113. New York: Teachers College, Columbia University, 1921.

Haviland, Virginia, and Smith, William Jay. *Children and Poetry.* Washington, D.C.: The Library of Congress, 1969.

Huber, Miriam B., Bruner, Herbert B., and Curry, Charles M. *Children's Interest in Poetry.* Chicago: Rand McNally and Company, 1927.

Huck, Charlotte S., and Kuhn, Doris Young. *Children's Literature in the Elementary School.* Holt, Rinehart and Winston, Inc., 1968.

Jordan, Arthur M. *Children's Interest in Reading.* Contributions to Education, No. 107. New York: Teachers College, Columbia University, 1921.

Kangley, Lucy. *Poetry Preferences in the Junior High School.* Contributions to Education, No. 758. New York: Teachers College, Columbia University, 1938.

Norvell, George W. *What Boys and Girls Like to Read.* New York: Silver Burdett Company, 1958.

Weekes, Blanche E. *The Influence of Meaning on Children's Choices of Poetry.* Contributions to Education, No. 354. New York: Teachers College, Columbia University, 1929.

Journal Articles

Avegno, T. Sylvia. "Intermediate-Grade Choices of Poetry." *Elementary English,* XXXIII (November 1956), pp. 428-432.

Bradshaw, Ruth E. "Children's Choices in the First Grade," *Elementary English Review,* XIV (May 1937), pp. 168-176, 188.

72 CHILDREN'S POETRY PREFERENCES

Coast, Alice B. "Children's Choices in Poetry as Affected by Teachers' Choices," *Elementary English Review*, V (May 1928), pp. 145-147, 159.

Eckert, Mollie H. "Children's Choices of Poems," *Elementary English Review*, V (June 1928), pp. 182-185, 192.

Grant, Emma B., and White, Margaret L. "A Study of Children's Choices of Reading Materials," *Teachers College Record*, XXVI (April 1925), pp. 671-678.

Hofer, Louise B. "What Do Sixth Graders Really Like in Poetry?" *Elementary English*, XXXIII (November 1956), pp. 433-438.

King, Cora. "Favorite Poems for Children of Elementary School Age," *Teachers College Record*, XXXIII (May 1922), pp. 255-273.

Kyte, George C. "Children's Reactions to Fifty Selected Poems," *Elementary School Journal*, XLVII (February 1947), pp. 331-339.

Mackintosh, Helen K. "A Critical Study of Children's Choices in Poetry," *University of Iowa Studies in Education*, VII, No. 4 (September 1932).

Mackintosh, Helen K. "A Study of Children's Choices in Poetry," *The Elementary English Review*, I (May 1924), pp. 85-89.

Nelson, Richard C. "Children's Poetry Preferences," *Elementary English*, XLIII (March 1966), pp. 247-251.

Wissler, Clark. "The Interest of Children in the Reading Work of the Elementary School," *Pedagogical Seminary*, V (1897-1898), pp. 523-540.

Unpublished Material

Tom, Chow Loy. "What Teachers Read to Pupils in the Middle Grades." Unpublished Ph.D. dissertation, The Ohio State University, 1969.